21ST-CENTURY PROSPECTING

The Authoritative Playbook for
New Business Development

John Rosso & Mark McGraw

Foreword by David Mattson

Print ISBN: 978-1-7370102-6-5

eBook ISBN: 978-1-7370102-5-8

This book is dedicated to your success

as a sales professional.

Contents

Acknowledgments

I owe so much to my dad Larry and my mom Jeanne. They provided a home of unconditional love and support. I want to thank my wife Catherine and my sons Jack, Steve and Joe, my daughter Cait, and my daughter-in-law Gretchen for their love and support.

This is my twenty-seventh year teaching Sandler. David Mattson, thank you for your leadership, and thanks to the home office team and the entire book production team for all the hard and often unrecognized work you do to support us. Thank you to the Sandler network of trainers. You are the lifeblood of the organization, always on a quest for constant and never-ending improvement. Thanks to my South Carolina team of Rusty Fox, Stephen Ross, Emily Yepes, Stevie Depew, and Sarah Blake.

A big thank-you to our committed and gutsy clients who make the world a better place by being gutsy five seconds at a time. Thank you to my friend and coauthor Mark McGraw and long-time accountability partner Jody Williamson. Thank you to David Sandler—I think you would be amazed at the success of Sandler training. Finally, a big thank-you to Yusuf Toropov, who so patiently took our words and crafted them into this book.

—John Rosso

I would like to thank the following people for helping to bring this book to life: David Sandler, the originator of the Sandler process—while I never met him in the flesh, his recordings have guided me for decades; Dave Mattson, for carrying on Sandler's legacy; John Rosso and Jody Williamson, who have been great partners in thinking; and the far-flung marketing and production team: Rachel Miller, Jamie Bernier, Kerri Martinek, Yusuf Toropov, Laura Matthews, Safie Maken Finlay, Margaret Stevens Jacks, Shannon Haaf Howell, Jena Heffernan, and Jerry Dorris. Most importantly, I thank my family, Devon, Katie and Jack, who bring me joy each day.

—Mark McGraw

Foreword

Thomas Watson, chairman and CEO of IBM in the first half of the 20th century, is credited with observing, "Nothing happens until somebody sells something." Although a lot of things have changed since he said that, his observation is just as true today as it was back then.

What has not been repeated quite as often, though, is the related and just as timeless fact that in most markets, nothing gets sold until somebody realizes that it's time to get busy and start prospecting. If you're reading these words, the odds are good that you are that somebody.

If you've ever said to yourself, "Where are the buyers, and how can I connect with them?" John Rosso and Mark McGraw wrote this book for you. It is all about creating enduring success at a high and sustainable level in today's market—not yesterday's. If you are ready to get busy and make things happen in today's buying environment, read on.

David Mattson
President/CEO, Sandler Training

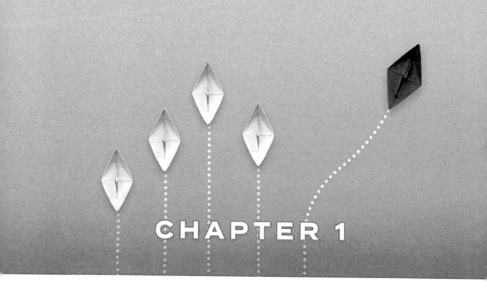

The Deal

In recent years, a whole lot has changed when it comes to prospecting for new business while some things have stayed the same. The trick is figuring out which is which.

Let's start with the changes all salespeople have to come to terms with. The dynamic of engaging with buyers is far different than it was just a few years ago. This is largely because of the seismic changes in the way people work and interact with one another that came about as a result of a global pandemic. It's far harder now to connect with people voice-to-voice if they haven't heard of you or your business before or if they have no frame of reference for an incoming call.

> The dynamic of engaging with buyers is far different than it was just a few years ago.

For a lot of decision makers, there are no longer any gatekeepers. They now do the job of screening for themselves. They are often overscheduled and hyper-focused on what they're doing. They move faster and have less time for distractions. As a result, they resolve to spend little to no time on the phone with people they don't know, and they tend to exclude anyone and everyone they consider irrelevant from their other communication channels.

All of this makes the idea of a "cold call" less tenable than it once was. At the same time, the core requirements of the interaction that must happen for sales professionals to turn an opportunity into a prospect remain the same. Despite the massive shifts that have taken place in the ways people now work and the technology they use to connect with each other, salespeople still have to accomplish exactly the same goals.

- Salespeople still need to establish some kind of bond with the other person and find a way to create and sustain rapport with them.
- Salespeople still need to set the agenda for what's going to happen during the interaction, and they need to do that in a way that makes sense to both sides.
- Salespeople still need to find a way to connect what they do to a problem or pain in the other person's world.
- And, of course, salespeople still need to get prospects to agree on a next step, so they can begin the process

of figuring out—together—whether it makes sense to do business.

The question is how to adapt to the radical changes that have taken place in the way decision makers work and, at the same time, fulfill everything that needs to happen to turn an opportunity (a lead) into a prospect.

What follows are these authors' answers to that question.

This Will Take You Out of Your Comfort Zone

Full disclosure: What we will be sharing with you in the pages that follow may, on occasion, feel a little uncomfortable at first. That's because the selling system here is designed to generate qualified prospects in this new selling environment.

You may be finding that what you're used to doing simply doesn't work as well as it did. This new environment demands a change in your personal prospecting paradigm. The operative word there is *personal.* This is not a book about sending out mass emails or setting up autoresponders. We are talking about shifting the way you think about your one-on-one interactions with prospective buyers. Make no mistake: The kind of shift we are talking about requires sustained effort over time, not a short burst of activity. It is all about building up and strengthening previously undeveloped sets of prospecting muscles.

Here is the deal we want to strike with you: At the end of each of the 34 chapters in this book, you will find a section entitled "Do This." For each working day after you start this book, if you complete one of the simple mini assignments outlined in the "Do This" sections, we promise that you will have a new set of prospecting muscles—and a paradigm shift that works in today's buying environment.

If you want that, you've come to the right place. But be aware: if you want that, you need to do the assignments!

- Do the assignment even if it feels strange.
- Do the assignment even if it takes you out of your comfort zone.
- Do the assignment even if no one else in your organization is doing it.

Keep that up for as many days as it takes to complete all 34 assignments. Not only will you have those new, strong muscles, but you will rock the competition. That's the deal.

Does that make sense? If it does, let's get started. We'll start with something ridiculously easy.

- Keep reading.

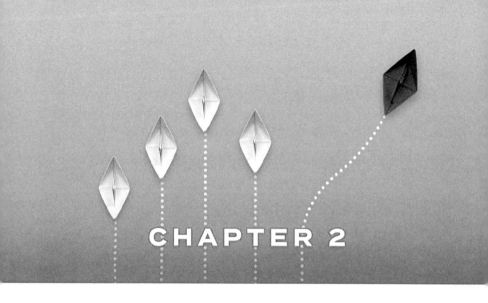

CHAPTER 2

What Makes Prospecting Success Happen?

Here's a question: When you think about what makes success happen in professional selling and prospecting, what words and phrases come to mind? What traits and habits do you think of?

Take a moment to think of some of those right now.

Perhaps you thought of words like *passion* and *confidence* and *sincerity* and *unstoppability*. Or perhaps you came up with *agenda-driven, goal-oriented,* or *alignment with buyers*. Or you could have thought of words like *persistence* and *execution*.

We've worked with a lot of sales professionals over the years, and we find that these are the kinds of words that show up when we ask this question. We'd be willing to bet that the word or words that just came to mind for you all fall into one of the three major "buckets" that define the areas in which we coach sales professionals to improve:

- Attitude
- Technique
- Behavior

We call these three elements, taken together, the Behavior/ Attitude/Technique (BAT) Triangle, otherwise known as the Success Triangle.

The Success Triangle

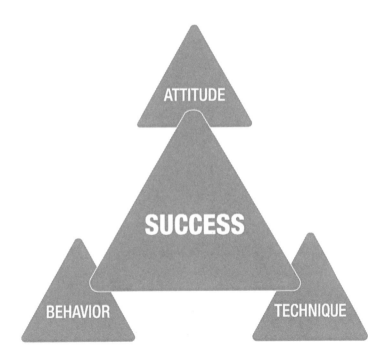

Attitude is your mindset, your beliefs, and your willingness to put yourself out there and take some risks. It's also your self-concept. Remember those words up above? Words like *passion* and *unstoppability* connect to your attitude. Attitude is essential, of course, but on its own it is not enough. You also need know-how.

Technique is basically the know-how that illuminates what to say and do—and how to say and do it. The abilities to *set the agenda* and *identify areas of alignment* with a prospective buyer connect to your technique.

Both of those points of the Success Triangle are vitally important, but the third, *behavior*, is essential. Even with great attitude and great technique, if you don't get out and do something, if you don't actually execute, nothing is going to happen. You have to "do the behaviors," as David Sandler, the founder of our company, was fond of saying. *Execution* and *persistence* connect to your behavior as a professional salesperson—to setting and implementing a plan that results in you hitting your goals.

The Keys to Success

The magical thing is, when you mix these three things together—behaviors, attitudes, and techniques—you can be successful at, really, anything. That sounds like an overstatement, but we promise you it's not. There's a reason we call these three points the Success Triangle. They really are capable of guiding anyone to success in any field of endeavor. They define success.

> Attitude, technique, and behavior are the
> three points of the Success Triangle.

So whether you are thinking about being successful in prospecting for new business (or your golf game or fly fishing or particle physics), the amazing thing is, by applying these same three principles, emulating successful people in your chosen field, and figuring out their attitudes, techniques, and behaviors, you, too, can be successful.

Of course, this book isn't about particle physics or fly fishing. It's all about giving you the tools you need to create and execute a plan for success in prospecting for new business in today's marketplace. It's cutting-edge. It's all about what will lead you to the fulfillment—and the over-fulfillment—of your goals right now in the 21st century. It's all about success in creating new business relationships on today's platforms, using today's technologies, and connecting with today's decision makers. As you make your way through this book, you're going to find that any meaningful success is rooted deeply in those three timeless principles: attitude, technique, and behavior.

On a separate sheet of paper or in a document on your phone or computer, rate yourself on a scale of 1–10 in terms of your current prospecting-related attitude, technique, and behavior.

- **Attitude.** A 10 in this area would mean you've typically got a lot of confidence—not arrogance, but confidence.

You are OK with rejection. If somebody rejects you, you're not sitting in the corner pouting—you bounce back fairly quickly. That's a 10 in terms of attitude. A 1 would be the complete lack of that kind of confidence.

- **Technique.** For this one, 10 means you know how to get meetings using today's technology. You know how to write effective messages that get responses through email. You know how to deliver a phenomenal 30-second commercial, in person or over the phone, that causes the prospect to cock their head and say, "Tell me more." You know how to deal with objections when you get them. Being able to do all of these things would be a 10. Having no ability in any of these areas would be a 1.

- **Behavior.** A 10 in this area means you've got a personal plan for your own long-term goals, short-term goals, and mid-range goals. You have a plan built out for each week knowing exactly the activities and quantities you need to do to get you to your goal—and you're doing it! Just as important, you know why you're doing it. A 10 means that you execute on the right behaviors consistently. Having no plan, or having a plan and not executing it at all, would be a 1.

Identify those scores, 1–10, in each of those three areas. Then, once you know the numbers, move on to the next chapter. There you will start to see what kind of progress you can make in all three of these areas.

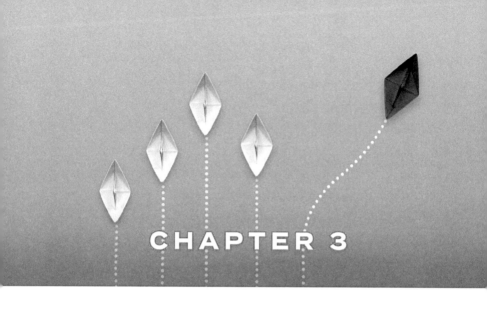

CHAPTER 3

The 21st-Century Paradigm Shift from Cold to Warm

This first and most important shift you need to make when it comes to prospecting effectively in the 21st century is a mental one.

This change in thinking concerns the kind of prospecting conversations you want to initiate with people. For decades, many professional salespeople operated under the assumption that one of their core responsibilities was approaching cold leads and turning them, through their charm, skill, and magnetic personality, into warm prospects. Every once in a while, of course, you might get a warm lead from a happy customer or a business ally, and that was nice enough when it happened, but the critical activity, in terms of techniques you learned and behavior you executed and measured, was the cold call. This changed somewhat when marketing started finding supposedly "warmer" leads in the digital era. Salespeople then knew that the person in question had requested a download or visited a certain article or done something else that made them fit a certain profile. But the truth remained that, even when you called someone who was supposedly warmer as a result of visiting your website or engaging in some other activity you liked, this was still a cold lead.

You still had to take a nonexistent relationship and find a way to warm it up because the person did not know you and had no reason to have a conversation with you. So that's what you did.

Everything changed after the global pandemic hit.

The New Reality

Now, we've been finding that with increasing reliance on digital platforms, with more people working in remote locations, with decision makers guarding their own calendars and their own productive time with a near-religious level of intensity, most of our clients report that cold calls, as conventionally understood, no longer make sense as the go-to weapon in the prospecting arsenal. The environment has changed. You need to change your paradigm if you expect to compete in the new environment.

Here is the first and most important shift in the paradigm:

The prospecting "job description" has changed. Today, the first and most important job for prospectors is to create warm leads, not to convert cold leads.

> Today, the prospecting job is, first and foremost, to create warm leads, not to convert cold leads.

The situation, in other words, has reversed. Previously, you might have spent most of your time generating opportunities by engaging with people you knew you had to warm up to initiate any kind of relationship. You expected only a few warm leads to come your way. Now it's the other way around. You must spend most of your time generating warm opportunities, and you should expect to convert few if any cold leads.

So how do you do that?

Our first answer is: Get a heck of a lot better at generating introductions and prioritize warm calls over cold calls. By the way, we prefer calling these all-important professional connections "introductions," rather than "referrals," even though most sales professionals still think in terms of referral generation rather than introduction generation. The reason? When you call it a referral, it sounds like you're a bad salesperson having trouble hitting quota. When you call it an introduction, it sounds like you're a professional who wants to add value. That second scenario is the mental image you always want to cultivate.

Are you ready for a paradigm shift? Are you ready to move from a prospecting plan based on cold conversations to one based on warm introductions?

Get Real

The global pandemic only brought into sharper focus a best practice that the most effective salespeople had already been following for a long time. Let's get real here: When it comes to prospecting, there's nothing better than a quality introduction from someone who knows you and loves you to someone who doesn't—yet.

Nothing warms up the sales process like a quality introduction. People are suddenly likelier to take your call, likelier to hear you out, and likelier to give you a next step. Introductions are where you want to be. However, most salespeople, in our experience, don't do a great job when it comes to generating these connections. Why is this?

As we see it, there are two main reasons. The first is that salespeople simply don't ask for introductions and have no set process for doing so. Why don't they ask? Because they think that asking will make the potential introducer uncomfortable. You've got to wonder how uncomfortable the person would be if you've been working with them for years, which is often the case. But this is what salespeople tell themselves.

The second reason is that, when they do ask for an introduction, they ask poorly. Typically, they just throw it out there, maybe at the end of a meeting, so it comes across as an afterthought. "Hey, by the way, if you ever come across anybody who might be interested in what we do, please let me know."

Of course, that call never comes.

Both of these reasons, in our view, are rooted in the salesperson's lack of confidence in starting the conversation about getting introductions. They typically have no viable process for doing this, and they feel uncertain about the whole issue.

When they are given a process, they are often given a lousy one that makes things more awkward and makes them less likely to ask for introductions. One of our clients told us they were taught to say this: "Who are three names of friends and family members whom I can talk to?" Then they were told to put the pen on the paper, look down at the paper, and not look up until the person across from them said some names. (Imagine someone sitting there doing this in the awkward silence, just peeking up once in a while. That's a lot of pressure.)

Fortunately, though, there is a much better process for generating quality introductions consistently—and you can master it. We'll share it with you in the next chapter.

Answer this question in writing:

- What is your current process for generating introductions (remember, that's a better word than "referrals")?

If you have such a process, outline it briefly and rate yourself, on a scale of 1 to 10, for how comfortable and confident you are in using it on a daily or weekly basis.

If you don't have a process that you execute consistently, write down "none."

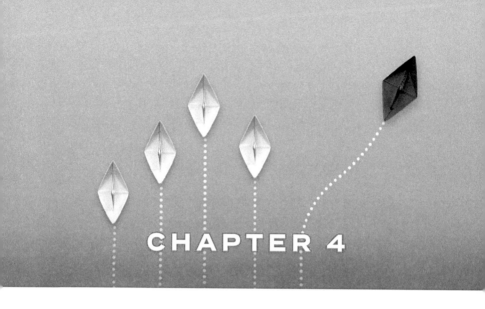

CHAPTER 4

The 4-Step
Process for Generating
Introductions

The process we are about to share with you can transform your month, your quarter, your year, and your career. It should be at or near the heart of your prospecting plan. Learn it! Practice it! Use it! Share it with your organization!

The 4-Step Process for Generating Introductions

There are four critical steps you need to follow when it comes to generating introductions. They are outlined below.

Step 1: Pick Your Introducers

Identify five people: five centers of influence, five clients, five friends. Pick the label that works for you. Whatever you call them, you want five folks you can see yourself having this discussion with. Write their names down. When you're done, move on to Step 2.

Step 2: Identify Value Transactions

Salespeople bring so much value to their current customer base. The big (and often unanswered) question is, how do they leverage that value?

Starting the conversation about introductions can begin with laying the groundwork for a value transaction. Maybe you've heard of something called the law of reciprocity: If you do something for them, there's an implied obligation that they should then want to do something for you. So you look for situations where you've already done something for the person. When somebody says, "Oh my gosh, Rory—that was so darn helpful," that's the start of a value transaction. By the way, if you know you've provided value and people haven't proactively mentioned it, you can always say, "Jade, let me ask you. Was this helpful?" When they say, "Oh my gosh, it was tremendous. Thank you so much," that's an acknowledgment of a value transaction.

That's a good way to think through who you want to talk to and how you want to approach the conversation. Don't limit yourself to the value that's been created after six months, a year, or two years, when you've already delivered all the results. In many cases, just by leading others through a sales process and discovery, you'll find you can start that value transaction.

So identify potential value transactions. Our guess is that you have a whole lot of these to choose from. Look for the areas where you have served and overserved each of the five people on your list. Write the examples down for each, and put a star by the example of highest value you delivered for each individual. For instance: Did you shorten someone's time to market? Did you reduce their employee turnover? Did you help them identify an inefficiency or an example of waste in one of their processes? Did you introduce them to someone who was able to help them achieve an important goal?

Only people to whom you've delivered significant value should show up on this list. If you need to revise your list to get it back up to five, do that.

Step 3: Plan Your Approach

An *approach* is a roadmap for a productive conversation. Just as you will have an approach for interacting with prospective buyers, you will want to develop an approach for interacting with clients and customers from whom you want introductions. And, you will want to write it down. In our experience, it's the lack of a written outline for this conversation that is the primary reason salespeople either don't start this discussion or execute it badly.

Consider the following approach. Review it closely, then use it as your model as you write one that feels natural to you.

> **You:** Jade, if you've got an extra minute or two, I'd like to ask you about something that's important. Do you have an extra minute or two?

Note that you're not saying, "Oh, by the way, do you know anybody who I might sell to?" That's a throwaway. If you want a listener to give their full attention, you don't start a conversation with "by the way." Instead, you introduce a topic, identify that it's important, and get a time commitment.

What's next? Think back to that value transaction. You've got this great relationship, you know you don't want to impose, but you do want to have the conversation. The thing to do is set up an agenda for the conversation you're about to have that leverages the value transaction in a subtle but unmistakable way. Establish an agreement about the purpose of the conversation, an agreement that references what you've done for this person. Again, this is not a hit-and-run, not a "by the way," but an important discussion that's worth setting up mutual understandings around. It could sound like this:

> **You:** Jade, I've been thinking. I know we've had a great relationship, and you've always been appreciative of the work we've done. If you're open to it, I'd like to take a few minutes to brainstorm with you and even perhaps create a short list of people who are in your network who you think may be open to our work and could be a good fit for the kind of things we do. Is that something you're comfortable with?

Let's focus in on a couple of key phrases that show up in what you just read. We really like the word "brainstorm" because it implies collaboration, which is what you're after. Another important phrase is: "...even perhaps create a short list of people in your network, who you think may be open to our work." We also like: "Is that something you're comfortable with?" That makes it clear that you're not trying to ram this down the person's throat. You're not demanding that they name three people and waiting with your pen on the sheet of paper.

Now the beauty of starting the conversation in this way is that if they say, "Honestly, Rory, it is not something I'm comfortable with. I just don't like to get into other people's business," you don't lose any relationship juice. You then get a chance to say, "Hey, Jade, that's why I asked. I appreciate you, and I appreciate the relationship. No worries."

But you know what? If you've actually delivered value to this person, that's probably not what you're going to hear. It's much more likely that they'll say something like, "Sure, that makes a whole lot of sense."

In which case, you'll continue by painting a picture for the other person.

Step 4: Paint a Picture

Continue by saying something like this:

You: Would it be helpful, Jade, if I painted a picture for you of the three or four types of people who typically are the best fit?

[Good news: We predict a 100% yes response to that question.]

Client: Sure.

You: Great. As I'm describing these types of people, if anyone comes to mind who fits these criteria, just jot the name down. That doesn't mean it will definitely make sense to introduce me. You and I can decide that later.

This takes all the pressure off. Again, notice that you are not forcing the person to answer you and demanding names. Why are you offering criteria rather than just suggesting that the person recite a list to you right now? Let's answer that question by posing another one. What are you having for dinner next Thursday night?

Maybe you're struggling to answer that question, as most people would. That confusion, that uncertainty, that disconnect, is what people feel when you ask them, "Hey, do you know of anyone I can talk to?" It's like asking what someone is having for dinner on a day they're not even thinking about yet. They don't know. It's not on their radar screen. So they're likely to say, "I really don't know. Tell you what, let me give that some thought, and I'll give you a call." Those are calls that never come. What you've got to do is tap into their brain by painting a picture and giving them some time to think.

Another key tactic used in this ask was the word "introduce." Start substituting the word "introduce" for "referral." Asking for a referral puts a lot of pressure on the other person. With a referral, the person is putting their reputation on the line for you. Some people will be willing to do that, but it's a risky ask. When you use the word "introduce" instead, it lowers the bar and makes it easier for them to take action.

The key to painting the picture is to focus on observable characteristics. For instance, if you're a financial planner, do not say, "So, Jade, do you know anybody who might be unhappy with the service they're getting from their current advisor?"

Think about it. You know a lot of people. You probably have no idea how happy or unhappy they are with their advisor. You may know if they've got a second home, you may know if they're on a second marriage, you may know if their kids are in college or are hoping to go to college, and you may know if they've recently gotten divorced. Someone could ask you about that stuff, and you'd have something intelligent to say. But if someone asks you how happy they are with a particular vendor in their lives, you most likely won't know. All you know is the observable characteristics.

Whatever those observable characteristics are, that's where you want the conversation to go. If you don't know what your ideal client looks like and what their observable characteristics are, this is an excellent time to hit pause and find out. Outline the three or four real, observable characteristics of your ideal customer that are likely to make the other person think, "OK, that makes sense. I know someone who fits that criteria."

Here's how the conversation might proceed:

You: [Briefly outline an observable characteristic of your ideal client.] Anybody come to mind? Anybody who it may make sense to talk to?

Don't rush it; slow down. Let them work on it. The key to making this a productive conversation is taking your time. If you do that, the conversation might proceed as follows:

> **Client:** Hmm...someone who has kids who are getting ready to go to college. I think Sienna Maxwell may be a good fit for you.
>
> **You:** Great. What should I know about Sienna?
>
> **Client:** [Shares something about Sienna.]
>
> **You:** Got it. Wonderful. Anyone else come to mind?

When they run out of folks who fit that criterion, you have the option of saying, "So, the second category of people who tend to be great fits is..." Our advice is that you only do that if it feels right. Whether you opt to do that or not, your goal is to slow this conversation down and play it out for as long as it feels comfortable to both of you. And yes, we're emphasizing the point that you slow this conversation down—we're repeating that. Why? Because our experience is that salespeople are not comfortable with silence.

You must be comfortable with silence in order for this conversation to produce results for you. You have to get out of your own comfort zone when it comes to giving the other person time to think. Guess what? Once you do, you will be astonished at the amount of revenue this kind of conversation can produce for you.

They say money doesn't grow on trees, but you know what? It actually does. It grows on introduction trees!

Money does grow on trees—introduction trees!

If you stop and think about the customers you've served, the value you've delivered, and some of the people your clients have already introduced to you, you can see that it is almost a moral obligation to identify all the other people you can serve and help. Think about that for a moment. If you don't brainstorm those names, those people are either not going to get a solution at all or they're going to be served by someone who is less capable than you are. You should not allow either of those outcomes if you can possibly avoid it.

- Familiarize yourself with the four steps laid out in this chapter.
- Write out your approach for generating introductions to new prospects.
- Then practice your approach. Find a manager, find a peer, or find a friend you can practice with. Get your pacing down, and learn to be comfortable with the silences. Get good at this!

What we have shared with you here is a tremendous way to deepen relationships, bring value to new contacts, and generate revenue. Most salespeople don't do it. Once you do, you will have an extraordinary competitive edge.

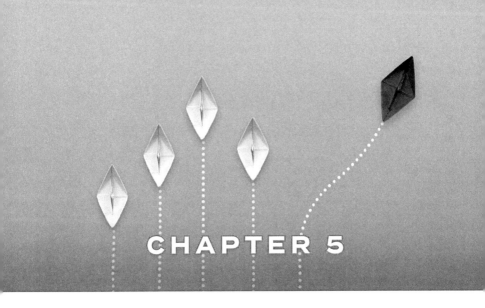

Five More Strategies to Generate Introductions

In the previous chapter, we looked in-depth at the kind of conversation you can map out and execute with current clients and customers to generate introductions to potential new prospects. That's an extremely powerful model. But it's not the only thing you can do to dramatically increase the number of warm introductions you get. Here are five more powerful strategies that will give you a significant competitive edge.

1. Look for Dandelions

You know what a dandelion is, of course. It's that plant that grows just about everywhere because its seed-distribution strategy is so perfect. A little wind comes up, the ripened dandelion shudders and waves, the puffy seeds detach, the breeze carries the seeds off in multiple directions, and, before you know it, a bunch more dandelions begin sprouting. Guess what? People are like dandelions. When someone you know leaves a company (for whatever reason) and lands somewhere else, that's an opportunity for you. When a decision maker—somebody who knows and likes you and who knows and likes your company—leaves Company A and is carried by the wind over to Company B, that's a reason for you to reach out and ask what they're working on. It might be a match.

You want to get good at noticing a dandelion whose seeds have been scattered to the wind, and you want to get good at tracking such dandelions down—either for yourself or for someone else in your organization. After all, the more of these you share with people on your selling team, the more likely you are to get a dandelion in return.

Most salespeople, in our experience, don't have very good dandelion-collection processes in place. Here are two simple, proven ways you can upgrade yours—and generate more warm conversations that can lead to new opportunities.

Put LinkedIn to work. LinkedIn calls its Sales Navigator application "the ultimate sales tool." That's some pretty intense marketing copy, we know. You may be tempted to dismiss such claims as over-the-top. Before you do, we advise you to give Sales Navigator a test drive. Sign up for, say, three months in support of your own personal "where are they now?" tracking system. There may be no better investment when it comes to tracking dandelions than the thousand dollars or so a year it costs to access and use this tool. We'll share just one example with you. Let's say you have a list of 75 people who love you, love what you do, and love your company. Wouldn't it be nice if you received an alert every time one of them left their current company? Wouldn't it be nice if you received an alert every time that person landed somewhere new? Of course it would. Make the case. Invest the thousand bucks. Start using LinkedIn's Sales Navigator to keep track of your dandelions.

While you're at it, you can also use the Sandler LinkedIn Levers tool, which can help you track down critical information about dandelions—and other contacts. You'll find it in the Appendix.

Do a Google search. Make a list of the top ten to twenty organizations you've worked with over the past three to five years—the success stories you are proudest of. Next, take the time to create a sublist of the key contacts you had at those organizations who have since moved on to other opportunities, people you've fallen out of touch with. Cross-check that list against your LinkedIn list of contacts. Do a Google search on anyone and everyone who doesn't have a LinkedIn profile. Do a little detective work. If they are working for an organization that looks like it could benefit from what you do, reach out, catch up on what's been going on, and find out if it makes sense to schedule a meeting. Even if it doesn't, you can use the process outlined in Chapter 4 to ask this person for an introduction.

2. Expand Your Wallet Share

What else does your best customer do that you could be helping with? What other projects are unfolding (perhaps in another department) that are running into, or are about to run into, problems you might be able to solve? Don't just fixate on the area where you are currently delivering value; expand your network of influence so you can uncover new, mutually beneficial opportunities. One great tool for doing this is Sandler's Quarterly Value Review (QVR) template, which you can use to schedule and lead quarterly "where are we now and where are we going" meetings with senior people at your client organizations. This is a simple two-page form that generates repeatable, high-level, client-facing events built around the twin concepts of "value delivered" and "value desired."

The whole point of the QVR is that, unlike the familiar quarterly business review (which is typically just a small-scale trade show), it's not about you. Rather, it's all about how the client defines and quantifies the value you've already delivered—and what the client needs to see from you next. There is no better platform for identifying new ways to add value and win more of the cash in your best account's budget. (You'll find a copy of the Quarterly Value Review Tool in the Appendix.)

3. Identify the Key Partnerships and Alliances

Someone who knows and loves you and your company is highly likely to be willing to introduce you to people at organizations that support and partner with them. So if the organization in question is large enough, you may want to ask about other entities—accountants, law firms, charitable organizations, foundations—that they're closely associated with. If it's appropriate, do the (minimal) research necessary to find out which of your client/customers' partnerships and alliances might have someone who has problems you can solve, and ask for an introduction.

4. Follow the Company's Family Tree

Are there affiliated organizations or sister companies that connect to a company or organization for which you have delivered results? If so, you can identify your current client's counterpart at that outfit and ask for an introduction. The beauty of this approach is that your current contact doesn't even need to know the person they are introducing you to.

5. Follow the Personal Family Tree

Whenever you can, using whatever available, appropriate, and legal resources you can, find out about the spouses or partners of your best contacts. Sometimes, that spouse will end up being in the same or a similar line of business and will be interested in hearing about how you have been able to solve parallel problems. It happens more often than you might think. When in doubt, ask for the introduction. What's the downside?

Frankly, that advice goes for all the introduction-generation techniques we've been sharing with you. When in doubt, find the right opportunity, the right time, and the right process to ask for the introduction—and then ask! Why on earth wouldn't you? If you want to start a fire, you use dry wood and find a dry place and get a pack of matches and some crumpled-up newspaper. Once you set everything up properly, all you need to do is strike the match. That's what asking for an introduction is like. Making a cold call in today's environment is a little like taking damp wood, piling it up in a soggy and cold spot, crouching down, and rubbing two sticks together for hours on end, hoping to ignite a spark. Could you start a fire that way? Sure. Is it a better investment of your time and energy to use the dry-wood-and-matches approach? Of course!

> Remember money goes on trees—introduction trees!

Think of every branch that comes off a tree as a person. As you get introductions to others off that branch, new branches form and the tree grows. At the end of every branch are sales that generate new relationships; new relationships bring new income.

DO THIS

- Identify at least 10 specific individuals you will reach out to, based on the strategies outlined in this chapter. (Feel free to make it more than 10 if you want.)
- Set up a subscription to LinkedIn Sales Navigator.
- Use the Sandler LinkedIn Levers Tool in the Appendix.

CHAPTER 6

One More Thought
on Introductions

By now, you've closely examined both your behaviors and your goals in terms of getting introductions. Before we leave that subject, we want to remind you to pay just as close attention to your giving goals.

This chapter is your reminder that you have to give more to get more. In other words, the people who are great at giving introductions are, reliably, the people who get the most introductions. So you want to devote some time to your giving plan too. If you get some introductions and you close some business using the ideas we've shared with you, that's tremendous. But just remember: You're not done yet! How are you going to reward and acknowledge the one who helped you?

> **What are your giving goals?**

Personal, Unexpected, and Significant

People appreciate things that are personal, unexpected, and significant to them. Make sure you set up something like that for the person who sent a good introduction—or multiple good introductions—your way. Of course, if you have an introduction that's appropriate to their world or to someone in your circle who might be able to help them, you want to make that connection. But what else can you do? How else can you create a touch point for them that is personal, unexpected, and significant? Is it a handwritten note or card? Is it a gift subscription to a magazine that fits their interests? Is it a call just to say thanks—with no other agenda, no ulterior motive? A short, personalized video to them letting them know how much they are appreciated? It's really up to you.

The point is, there is something you can do to acknowledge and reward this person, something that serves the relationship and doesn't violate ethical, policy, or legal guidelines. Your mission is to identify that something—and then do it. You'll build a long-lasting bond with that person. You know what? They'll appreciate it, and they'll look for ways to show that appreciation. At some point, you'll get a call from them and hear them say, "I thought about somebody else I think you can help." That's how the introduction tree grows.

- Set up a plan for acknowledging and rewarding the people who send good introductions your way. Execute on that plan.

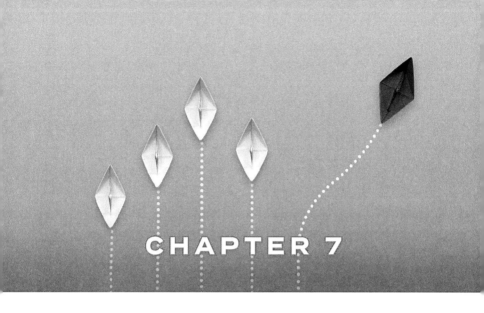

CHAPTER 7

The Foundation Skill

There are lots of different ways to hold prospecting conversations in the 21st century and lots of different platforms you can use to develop the relationships you need to hit your goals. But there is no way to prospect effectively if you haven't mastered one critical skill: the skill of engaging, connecting with, and motivating someone else, voice-to-voice in real time, to make a space on their calendar for a more in-depth conversation with you. If you can't have that conversation, an introduction isn't going to do you a whole lot of good.

So what we're going to be looking at next, and at some length, is the architecture of that initial conversation, typically conducted via a telephone or video call. We call that the "approach call."

The quality of your approach call supports everything else in your prospecting plan. Once you master that core skill, you can add all the other strategies and leverage all the different platforms that support effective prospecting. The ability to deliver that approach call professionally and consistently is what empowers you to set up a powerful, state-of-the-art, 21st-century prospecting plan.

That plan is going to be all about hybrid selling. The big idea is that you want to be adaptable. You want to be just as effective in digital platforms as you are in voice-to-voice or face-to-face meetings. In our view, this starts with designing, mastering, and delivering the right approach call. This is omni-channel prospecting. Some people are going to want to interact with you voice-to-voice. Some people are going to want to interact with you via email. Some are going to want to interact via text messages. Once you have the skills to hit all the marks to generate a live conversation, you can hit the same marks in conversations that take place in other platforms—but not before.

> Your plan is going to be all about hybrid selling. You want to be just as effective in digital platforms as you are in voice-to-voice or face-to-face meetings.

So let's spend some time looking at what goes into an effective approach call—perhaps a call to someone you've been introduced to, perhaps a call to someone else. What does that call look and sound like?

Pretend It's You

Let's say you're the prospect. You're sitting there in your mahogany-lined office, feet up on the desk, reading *Widget Weekly*, when a phone call comes in.

You pick it up, and it's a salesperson.

Be honest. What goes through your mind?

If you haven't asked yourself this question before, it's time to ask it now. Think about what actually goes through your prospect's mind. They've had these calls before—even you have had these calls before. How are you going to feel when you know that you've got a call from a salesperson to navigate?

Answer: Not great. You are going to want to wrap the call up—and the quicker, the better. Or, better yet, dodge it altogether. Right?

Here is the point: If you look, feel, and act like a stereotypical salesperson, you can expect to be treated like one. Unfortunately, if they don't know anything about you and they decide that you look, feel, and act like a stereotypical salesperson, they will not trust you.

So the question is, how do you change that dynamic?

Let's be blunt. All the salespeople who have talked to this person before have not done you any favors in terms of image-building. Most of their calls were, shall we say, not effective. Salespeople show up and throw up, right? They blurt out everything they can do with their wonderful new Model X in 30 seconds—and then the other person hangs up.

You can imagine the tension building. That's why you know folks are looking to get off the phone call. That's why you hear things like this:

Prospect: You know what, you caught me in the middle of a meeting.

Seriously? They're in the middle of a meeting, and they're going to pick up a random dial? That doesn't make sense. What they're really saying is this:

Prospect: I've been down this road before and I don't want to go down this road with you, but I'm too polite to say that.

What you want to do is undo the damage done by everyone who has gone before you. Your aim is to be 180 degrees different than the last call they received. In the following chapters, we're going to take you through the structure of an effective approach call—which is another way of describing a call that changes the game, breaks the rules, and empowers you to get the appointment.

You must break the ineffective rules. You must change the paradigm. You must get away from the tactics that haven't been working, the stereotypes that are waiting to undermine you within seconds of the other person picking up the phone.

It's time to start looking at how to do just that. Spoiler alert: A lot of up-front work goes into getting this conversation just right. Be prepared to do that work. Most salespeople don't do the level of preparation that we will be asking you to do. They "wing it." That's why prospects lean away from those conversations.

- Move on to the next chapter.

CHAPTER 8

Three Big Mistakes You Want to Avoid

[Ring, ring, ring.]

Prospect [answering phone]: This is Kebe.

You: Oh, hey, Kebe. Sterling Norris here at Technical Creations. How are you today?

Guess what? That "How are you today?" just killed the conversation.

What Prospects HAYT

How many times have you heard "How are you today?" from a salesperson—and instantly disengaged from the call? Countless times, right? That should tell you something. It should tell you that there are big mistakes that can betray you in the prospecting call and that it is your job to identify them and avoid them.

"How are you today?" is one of those mistakes. It's a verbal tic. Salespeople rely on it, even though they know that it pulls the energy and focus out of any prospecting conversation. How many times have you said that and you've heard the energy dip? The other person thinks: *Oh my gosh. It's a prospecting call.* And you hear:

Prospect: Yeah, fine, what do you have for me?

Or, worse yet:

Prospect: [Click.]

So that's the first prospecting mistake we want to avoid: "How Are You Today"—also known as "HAYT." Prospects HAYT that!

Don't Get All Singsongy

On any prospecting call, it's vitally important to listen to your tonality. A lot of tonality comes across as singsongy. Here's an example of what singsongy sounds like: "Oh, *hey,* Kebe, Sterling *Norris* here at Technical *Creations.* How are *you* today?"

Avoid the singsongy-ness; it's a tell. It tells the other person that you are in fact a salesperson. It reveals to them that even though they don't know you, they are free to rely on their stereotypes of what salespeople are like because you're doing that thing salespeople do. It tells them that they should raise the defense walls.

Keep your tonality steady, low, confident, and professional-sounding. Don't get all singsongy.

Avoid the "Mother May I" Road

Going down the "Mother May I" road means acting like you're less than the other person. You're not.

When you go down that road, you might often find that you're using words like "just":

You: I'm just following up/I just wanted to check in/I just wanted to spend a couple of minutes.../I just wanted to see if...

Why do you need the word "just"? That minimizes you. Be "unjust"!

What's happening with that word is that you're subordinating yourself, from a psychological point of view, to the other person. That's unprofessional.

As a professional, always look for ways to develop equal business stature. Remember, it's an equal-opportunity planet. You have a right to be here. Act like it.

- Banish the phrase "How are you today?" from your prospecting vocabulary—in any and every communication platform.

- Record and listen to your typical prospecting approach. Is it singsongy? If so, change your tonality.
- Resolve never to go down the "Mother May I" road.
- Make a list right now of other verbal tics that may be betraying you during prospecting calls and that may be causing you to lose your edge. Share that list with your coworkers and your manager. Let them review it and give you feedback. With their help, identify other areas where you may be reminding prospects of the typical salesperson—and find a way not to.

CHAPTER 9

Begin with a Pattern Interrupt

You walk into a store, and an eager, young salesperson trots up to you and says, "Can I help you?"

You say, "No, thanks, I'm just looking."

How long did you have to think about that response?

A fraction of a second, right? You might even have been tempted to say it before the salesperson could get the words "Can I help you?" out!

That's what you could call a conditioned response. Even if you went in there specifically knowing what you wanted to buy, you didn't want to be bothered by a salesperson. So you said you were just looking. And there was no connection.

Why, then, as a professional salesperson, would you choose to start a conversation in that way?

Beginnings and endings matter. If you can get the train on the right track, your odds of getting to the destination go way up. So ask yourself, how do you get around the conditioned response?

You might've heard of Pavlov's dogs—maybe that name rings a bell. (Get it?) Professional salespeople have to address the Pavlov problem. They've got to deal with the conditioning that's already there—to break the conditioning. The minute the other person picks up the phone, the conversation is like a garage door descending. You've only got about four, six, eight seconds to hit the button that will reverse the motor and lift up the defense wall. You're not going to do that by saying, "How are you today?" or by soliciting any kind of conditioned response. Let's face facts: If a call doesn't start well, it's probably not going to end well.

However, if you can put the train on the right tracks at the beginning, you have a much better chance of reaching the desired destination at the end of the call: the happy outcome of setting the appointment. How do you make that happen?

You do it by opening the discussion with something we call a *pattern interrupt*. A pattern interrupt is basically a way to shake things up. To be different. To sound unique. To quietly subvert and challenge what the other person expects is going to happen during the call.

Now, fair warning—pattern interrupts are, by design, meant

to be different. That means they may take you out of your comfort zone. They might throw you off at first. One thing that we've learned in our years of coaching is that, in pattern interrupts as in everything else, you have to find something that works for you. We're going to present a few different examples of pattern interrupts so that you can find the one that fits your personal style. We know this is not a one-size-fits-all situation. We want to help you discover or adapt an opening that works for you.

Here are four possible pattern interrupts you may want to consider for the opening of your discussion.

"I Promised..."

The pattern interrupt you use when reaching out to someone you've been given an introduction to is important to design and execute carefully. You may not think that a pattern interrupt is even necessary in the situation because this is a warm call rather than a cold call, but consider this: It is definitely possible to crash and burn on these calls—and far too many salespeople do. Why? They squander their leverage.

You squander your leverage by saying things like, "Hey Steve, I got your name from Fiona."

"I got your name." Think about what that phrase does. If you are on the other end of this call, are you eager to pursue this conversation when you hear that? Probably not. The caller stumbled upon your name in passing while talking to Fiona and instantly thought they could hit you up for a sale. You've heard this kind of thing before. You start thinking, *This is a sales-person who's behind quota*. It could have been a conversation between peers, but all of a sudden, it's a conversation between people who are at very different levels. If you use that tactic as the caller, you have lost all your leverage.

But suppose you were to say something like this instead:

[Ring, ring, ring.]

Prospect: This is Bruno.

You: Hey, Bruno, Midori Franklin here. Had a nice conversation with Jacob Silverman over at Silverman International. He and I got around to talking about the work that you two do together. He thought it might be important that we speak. I promised him that I would reach out to you.

Think about how differently you have positioned yourself with this opening. You are calling as a way to follow through on a commitment you made. Isn't that what professionals do? You could even leave that on the voicemail, and you will likely get a call back.

> Don't squander your leverage.

Here's another more lighthearted pattern interrupt you can use in this situation:

[Ring, ring.]

Prospect: This is Bruno.

You: Hey, Bruno, Midori Franklin here. I had a nice conversation with Jacob Silverman. He thought it might make sense for you and I to speak. Question for you: Do you even admit to knowing Jacob in public?

Timing is everything with this one. If you execute it properly, which may take a little practice and is dependent somewhat on the personalities involved, everyone laughs. The tension goes down, and the conversation moves forward.

What you are establishing with either of these techniques is that all-important element known as equal business stature. You are not asking for any favors. You are not begging. You are on an equal level with the person you are calling. That equality needs to be there throughout the call and throughout the sales cycle.

"Help Me If You Can..."

Another pattern interrupt that we like is:

You: Hey, I'm looking for some help.

What would happen if, when you called somebody, you struggled a little bit on the front end and maybe asked for their assistance? You can extend this in a way that feels comfortable for you. For instance: "Hey, Nila, it's Rowan over at Two Tiers. Listen, I'm looking for some help. Not sure if you could lend me a hand here for a minute. Is that possible?" What would happen if, after you said that, you just waited for the response?

More often than you might expect, you'll find yourself on the right track. You'll hear the other person say something like, "What can I do for you, Rowan?"

What we've found (and what tens of thousands of Sandler

clients have found) is that if you struggle a little bit, a lot of times that's enough of a pattern interrupt. It catches people off guard. Their natural human compassion kicks in. They aren't even thinking about the stereotypes. They want to help you, and they want to assist you. And all of a sudden, you've got a conversation.

Silence Is Golden

This one is kind of weird, but it works for us. We like it. You may not. Your call—you be the judge and you decide.

Often, if you're making a call to somebody, you can actually just call and use silence as a pattern interrupt after saying your name and your company. It sounds like this:

You: Hey, Phil, it's Violet Sirocco at Heavenly Slumber.

Then you just...wait.

Yes, there's an awkward pause. That awkward pause causes them to think to themselves, "Hey, do I know this person?" And very often (not always, but very often), in a twist on the stereotype, they'll say, "Hey Violet, how can I help you?" But this time, with them saying it, there you are, on the right track.

Setting Up a Punch Line

Here's another example of a pattern interrupt that you may want to consider. This one depends on who you're calling. If you're calling engineers, computer scientists, or other highly analytical types, you may not want to use this, but if you're calling a marketing- or sales-oriented person, you may have some success with it.

Prospect: This is Fumiko.

You: Hey, Fumiko. This is Eduardo Mason. Fumiko, if I told you I was making a cold call, would you want to hang up?

Prospect: Probably.

You: Well, in that case I'm glad I didn't tell you I was making a cold call.

Fumiko laughs. You laugh. Laughter is good. Suddenly there's a conversation.

Which Is Right for You?

As you evaluate these options, think about putting the train on the tracks. You've put the train on the tracks in a good way when the person you're calling asks how they can help you. These pattern interrupts create the opportunity for you to change the dynamic in a positive way, right from the very beginning—definitely something to consider.

- There are all kinds of different things you can say or do to create pattern interrupts. We've pointed you toward four. Identify and adapt at least two that work for you. What's something you've read here that you can make your own, then use consistently and reliably? What's something that instantly reverses the expectations on the other side, something that fits with your personality, something that will help you put the train on the tracks from the very beginning and start the call off the right way?

- In particular, select and practice the pattern interrupt you will use at the beginning of a call for which you've been given a warm introduction to someone.

- Resolve not to squander your leverage, not to squander that equal business stature, not to squander the chance to make people feel comfortable talking to you. Make that a professional commitment. And then follow through on it.

CHAPTER 10

The Mini Up-Front Contract

In sales, as in everything else of importance, you want to begin with the end in mind. That means you want to inspect what you expect.

In other words, you want to ask a question that not enough salespeople ask: How do you set the right ground rules for this approach call you're making? What, exactly, do you expect from the interaction?

Recall that the first step of the approach call is the pattern interrupt. What's the second step? It's setting what we at Sandler call a mini up-front contract. This will always follow your pattern interrupt. An up-front contract is a verbal agreement with the prospect about what you and they can expect to take place in a few key areas: time, agenda, and outcome. We call it a mini up-front contract because it's a condensed version of the kind of verbal contract you'd set with someone you were having a deeper conversation with (more details on this later).

> Inspect what you expect.

This contract is pretty simple. It's setting the stage; it's helping your prospect understand where this is going, and it's letting them know that you're looking to make a decision, even if that decision is only to talk further. So here are a couple of examples of a mini up-front contract, an agreement to set in advance with the prospect to set expectations for the call.

> **You:** Shani, I'm reaching out to you for two specific reasons. Let me share with you what they are. And then, you and I can decide whether it makes sense to talk further. Fair enough?

What happens when you say "two specific reasons"? When your prospect hears that, don't you think they're going to be curious about what those reasons are? Aren't you curious already? Your prospect will be too. They want to know what those reasons are. Just as important, they know that there is a purpose to this call and that by talking to you, they can figure out just what it is.

Here's an example that's a little simpler.

You: Shani, let me tell you the reason I am calling. And then, you and I can decide whether it make sense for us to sit down together at some point. Fair enough?

In both of these, notice what you're doing: You're setting the ground rules, as one professional talking to another. By the way, it's extremely important to deliver the mini up-front contract with a confident tonality, with the voice of authority. (Remember what we said earlier about equal business stature?)

And here's another variation:

You: Hey, Shani, why don't I take 30 seconds and tell you the purpose of my call, and then you can decide where we take it from there. Fair?

Make the First Sale

Essentially, what you're doing with this step of the approach is making a sale. And it's got to be a quick sale. You have about eight seconds, max, to set the contract and use that contract to sell a three- to five-minute conversation.

> Your goal is to use the eight precious seconds that come after the pattern interrupt to sell a three- to five-minute conversation.

Now, if your tonality is good, you should close that sale 90% of the time or better. Skeptical? Don't be! When you deliver this properly, as one professional talking to another, nine out of ten people will agree to complete the approach call with you.

They will say something like, "Sure," "OK, that makes sense," or "What's on your mind?"

- Look closely at the examples of mini up-front contracts that we've shared with you in this chapter. Pick one that works for you.
- Write it down, using words that feel right to you—but do hold on to that word "fair" because it's important. Then practice the contract by saying it out loud five times.
- When you feel comfortable with it, begin to put it together with your pattern interrupt. Say that out loud five times. Time yourself. You should be able to deliver both within 15 seconds or less to set the stage for a quality three- to five-minute conversation.

Pain
Statements

The goal of the mini up-front contract is to create an
environment where you can deliver the next step—the
30-second commercial for your organization—without feeling
you have to rush to get through it. You're buying yourself that
time and getting that agreement to move forward—together—
so you can deliver a powerful summary of what you do and
who you do it for in a confident, measured, authoritative way.

This brings us to the question: What goes into that 30-second
commercial? And, just as important, what shouldn't go into it?

Permission to speak freely? Thanks. All right, brace yourself.

Here it is. People don't care about what you sell. At the end of the day, they simply don't care about the product or service that you're providing.

Yes, that's harsh. No, it may not be what your marketing department is used to hearing. Yes, it is the most important thing to understand when it comes to putting together a 30-second commercial that makes someone sit up, take notice, and hear you out for long enough to decide whether you are actually worth scheduling time with.

What people care about is the pain or problem that your product or service can help them disappear, sooner rather than later.

> People don't care about the product or service that you're providing. They care about the pain or problem that you can help them disappear.

That's what they're buying—a fix to a problem they have—and that's what they're going to be most intrigued about. That's what's going to persuade them to meet with you and discuss the possibility of doing business together—their pain and whether you can make it go away.

A lot of times when salespeople sell, they're trying to pitch their product or service. Therefore, they tell people what they do. The challenge is that prospects are not going to relate to that. In fact, they push back from it. The more you talk about what you do, the more likely they are to feel like you're selling to them. And that's a problem. People love to buy, but they hate people selling to them.

> People love to buy, but they hate being sold
> to. They buy for their reasons—and these are
> often in spite of the salesperson's reasons.

They don't care that you were founded in 1954 or that you've won XYZ award or that you use reinforced kryptonite on your production line. Stay away from all of that.

The Heavy Lifting

Let's talk about the heavy lifting. It's time to dig in and create the template that you'll use to talk with prospective buyers. One thing to remember is that people buy for their reasons, not yours. Another thing to bear in mind is that pain is a far better motivator than pleasure. Which would you put more effort into: Earning $1,000 within 24 hours or not losing $1,000 within 24 hours? The second one, right? That's because avoiding pain and loss and moving away from a negative consequence is a far stronger motivator than pleasure. That's just a given with human behavior.

In your conversations, therefore, you want to focus on the current pain—not some future pleasure and definitely not your product or service. You want to practice delivering your best condensed summary of that pain, right out loud, until you get it just right.

As a sales professional, whenever you're focused on your product as opposed to their pain, you lose. You've got to turn that around. In order to construct an effective 30-second commercial that includes the kinds of the problems you fix, which will get your listener to engage emotionally with you, you have to create a series of brief summaries that we call *pain statements*.

The best way we've found to coach this and to help you create pain statements is an acronym that sounds a little funny at first: FUDWACA.

If you've never read that word before, you're probably thinking to yourself, *What the heck does that mean?* It's not so much what it means but what each letter stands for. F-U-D-W-A-C-A: Each one of those letters stands for an emotional word that may connect to something the other person is feeling about a problem that you could help them fix.

Let's start with an example of someone providing computer repair, computer maintenance and service, and computer security. What problems does that person have solutions for, and, just as important, how do that person's customers feel about those problems? Well, those customers might well be:

- **Frustrated** with lost productivity.
- **Upset** about a particular disgruntled former employee's ongoing access to sensitive customer information.
- **Disappointed** about the performance of the current antivirus software.
- **Worried** about whether they've done enough to prevent a ransomware attack.
- **Angry** about losing proprietary data when an employee leaves and takes unauthorized materials with them.
- **Concerned** about the possibility of hackers shutting down their business.
- **Anxious** about security risks they just saw in the news.

See what we mean? The nonsense word FUDWACA—which is pretty much useless for anything else—does a great job of helping you remember those seven powerful emotional states.

> FUDWACA reminds you of seven
> powerful emotional states.

Each FUDWACA term is an emotional word that connects with a problem that your product or service is going to help fix. Now that you know that—and you know what the words are—let's get to work.

An executive we know once asked the question, "How much would you rehearse if you were getting paid $500,000 to deliver a 30-second monologue on your favorite TV show?" Quite a bit, right? That high level of practice is important to commit to for this conversation. Why? Because the default setting for salespeople is to talk about their product or service. Many salespeople have been doing that for years. It's time to reverse that programming.

Are you ready to begin that process?

- Think about someone you will be calling. What are their titles? Who is the ideal contact when it comes to buying and advocating for your solution? Are you calling a CEO? Are you calling a director of administration at a hospital? Are you calling a quality control specialist at a manufacturing company? Are you calling a chief revenue officer at a company that employs between a hundred and two hundred people? Are you calling the head of accounting at a company with a dozen or so people? What is the specific role of the person you most want to talk to? How big is the organization they work for? Think about the specific people who you're going to be speaking with.

- Next, think about the problems they have in their life that if you were working with them, those problems would lessen or disappear.

- Next, take a few minutes to write down some statements that describe the emotional impact of the pain or problems that you and your organization can help these people solve. For instance: "They're worried that they are vulnerable to a cyber ransom attack."

- Come up with five to seven statements. Start with a FUDWACA word—frustrated, upset, disappointed, worried, angry, concerned, anxious—and work from there until you have a half dozen or so brief pain-related statements that would draw out the prospect and make them think (or say), "Yeah, that's how I feel." Be sure to focus on the pain or problem you would help them fix in their life. Remember, this is not about your products, not about your services, not about your features and your benefits, at least not yet. Your job right now is to put the pause on the product training and write five to seven problems that a specific kind of prospect has in their life that you can solve—each of which builds on one of those powerful FUDWACA words.

- Then practice delivering those statements, right out loud.

CHAPTER 12

Drafting
Your 30-Second
Commercial

Have you ever been asked at a party "What do you do for a living?" and found yourself just wandering through the desert? Meaning, you start to answer the question, realize you've been talking for longer than you meant to, and notice that the other person's eyes are glazing over?

Same phenomenon, different situation: Have you ever been on a call and realized that your 30-second commercial has somehow turned into a three-minute documentary? What do you imagine the person on the other end of the call is doing when that happens? Basically, the same thing as the person at the party. Their eyes are rolling in the back of their head, they're falling asleep, or they're checking Twitter.

How do you avoid getting lost like that? How do you avoid the scenario where you find yourself wandering aimlessly through your own verbiage—and the other person tunes out?

In this chapter, we will give you the structure for a simple, powerful 30-second commercial that will keep you on track, keep you out of the desert, and get you where you need to be. We'll share some variations later on. But for now, we're going to keep it simple.

4 Steps to a 30-Second Commercial

This 30-second commercial can be broken down into four simple steps. Notice that this commercial comes after your pattern interrupt and your mini up-front contract.

Step 1. Introduction

Start with an introduction. This should describe who you typically work with and add value to. Think about which roles in a company you generally work with. Who are you contacting? Which customers benefit most from working with you? Are they directors? Directors of marketing? VPs of sales, or presidents, CEOs? Those would all fall under Step 1, the introduction. Then, transition seamlessly into the next step.

Step 2. Pain

For the second step of a 30-second commercial, it's time to go into the pain statements. In the previous chapter, you'll recall that you looked at the FUDWACA words and that you came up with some pain statements. Those will come in handy here. You can blend them into Step 2 as a part of your 30-second commercial. Of course, you can improve them as you go along.

If you're looking for examples of good pain statements, we can help you there. Let's say you are selling industrial equipment. In a situation like that, maybe you're calling on somebody who is a manufacturing supervisor or a manager. You might say this:

> **You:** We're working with manufacturing managers who in some cases are frustrated because they're experiencing poor service from their current suppliers. [Pause.] In other cases, they're disappointed with the reliability of the equipment. [Pause.] Maybe they also have some level of concern over their ability to upgrade the software through the system.

Notice that you built three pain statements into one smooth paragraph. Notice, too, that each pain statement should contain a FUDWACA word. Finally, notice that you've built in brief pauses to give prospects time to feel if they can relate. That's important.

Step 3. Benefit

Step 3 in your 30-second commercial is going to be the benefit statement. This is where you want to put in the *how* of the solution—how you will go about making the pain disappear. This step is optional. You can briefly include a benefit if you so choose.

Step 4. Hook

Step 4, and this is critical, ends the commercial with what we call a *hook question*. This kind of question is designed to get the other person to start to talk. You always want to end your 30-second commercial with a question that turns your little monologue into a dialogue, and you always want to do that as seamlessly as possible.

Designing this question properly is very important and so is practicing it until it sounds natural and confident. For example, you might say at the end of your 30-second commercial:

You: Are any of those issues familiar to you?

You: Are any of these things you're struggling with?

You: Does anything I'm saying here resonate with you?

An advanced version of the hook question, one that subtly encourages the other person to correct you (and forward the conversation), sounds like this:

You: I'm guessing you've got all of that under control. [Then, wait for a response. In fact, an awkward pause is exactly what you want. Let the other person respond. Remember, your goal is to get a conversation started.]

In a separate document or by filling out the form called 30-Second Commercial Creator that you'll find in the Appendix, create an initial draft of your calling approach. The four steps are listed below. Write words that work for you for each step.

- Create a first-draft introduction that says who you are, who you work for, and who you have been working with.

- Create a pain statement using one, two, or three problems you specialize in helping people remove from their lives. Use FUDWACA words for each pain.

- Write a brief benefit statement that says how you will solve the pain. No more than one sentence, please! (This step is optional.)

- Build a hook question that fits well for you and asks the person whether or not they're experiencing any of the pain statements you brought up in Step 2.

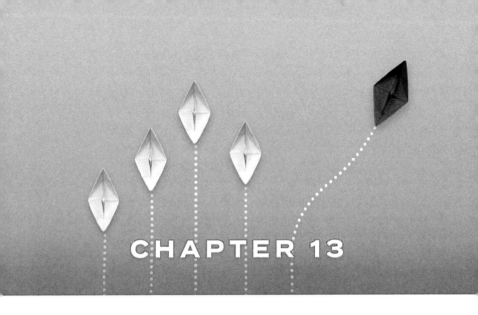

CHAPTER 13

Refining Your 30-Second Commercial

This is the shortest chapter in the book.

Take It Out for a Test Drive

All we want you to do right now is take that draft version of your 30-second commercial out for a test drive—and tweak it as necessary. The instructions you'll need to do this appear below.

- Set aside at least 10 minutes of private, uninterrupted time, so you can speak, record, and listen to your own 30-second commercial multiple times. Each time you listen to the playback, ask yourself the following questions:

  - "What could I do to make this sound more like me?"
  - "What could I do to make this more concise?"
  - "What could I do to make this easier for people to understand and respond to?"

- Every time you come up with an answer to one of those questions, revise the written draft of the call approach. Don't change the structure; don't put things in a different order; avoid the temptation to turn this into a long speech. Just look for ways to make it more authentic to you, tighter, and easier to understand.

- Once you have a second draft that you feel good about, move on to the next chapter.

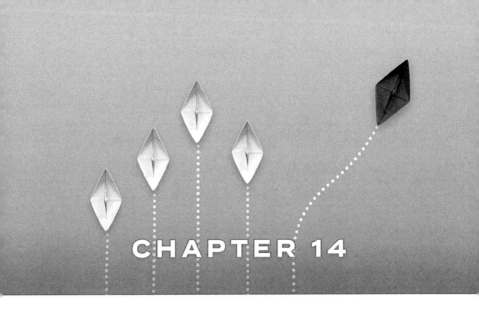

CHAPTER 14

Amp It Up with Third-Party Stories and Impact

Welcome back. By now you've created both a first and a second draft of your 30-second commercial, and you've read your draft out loud multiple times and revised it so that it feels comfortable to you. (If for some reason you haven't yet done those things, please do them.) In this chapter, you are going to ramp that up and amp it up. We are going to help you to give your 30-second commercial a bit more conversational impact.

To do that, we're going to introduce you to a powerful concept called *third-party stories*. A third-party story is what you use when you refer to the experiences of other people who face pains that are comparable to the business pain faced by the person you're calling.

During the prospecting call, you don't want to ask directly: "Are you having trouble with poor service, with reliability, with late deliveries, with [whatever]?" That's what we call a second-party question—a question about the prospect, or the "you" in the call that you're making. (A first-party question would be all about "me," or you in this call, which is obviously something to avoid.) Second-party questions are difficult to use because prospects think they're a trap. They are deeply wary about answering a question that sounds like it might as well be coming from a parent or authority figure. They don't know you that well yet, and they don't see any reason to open up to you when you put the pressure on like that. Who can blame them?

What you want to tap into is what's known as *social proof*. The idea here is pretty simple. It's to help the prospect think, "If others struggled with X, Y, and Z, it might be OK for me to talk about my struggles with those things." Third-party stories are easier to agree with and easier to talk about. You want to give people a chance to acknowledge that some of these challenges might affect them too, and you want to make it easier for them to take part in a conversation about those challenges.

The goal here is to take a close look at your pain statements and make sure they're phrased as third-party questions rather than second-party questions. You also want to arrange them in such a way that they highlight an impact that the person you're talking to will definitely be able to relate to.

So here is an example. Notice how it concludes with an impact—the answer to the question, "So what?"

> **You:** We do a lot of work with manufacturing managers who sometimes tell me they struggle with things like poor service, and that's a concern for them. Maybe they're frustrated because they're not getting return phone calls quickly enough. What they find is that, because of delays, they're not fixing the problem in a timely manner, and now the work product is going out the back door late. This is upsetting to them because it affects customer relationships.

That last one, as you may have noticed, is an impact. Here's another one:

> **You:** We talk to a lot of your counterparts at other manufacturing companies. Sometimes they tell me they're frustrated about back-ordered parts. They put them on order, they get a lead time, but soon they find that it's three days after that lead time date and they've still not received the parts. That's concerning because now they've got equipment downtime and they're paying employees who have no equipment to work on.

Again, that last piece is the impact. The impacts are what get the sale done.

Impacts get it done.

Turbocharge It!

It's time to start turbocharging your 30-second commercial. The way to do that is to make it conversational, to get in the head of your buyer, to make sure you're expressing pains in the form of third-party stories, and then to highlight the impact in a way that is going to be relevant to the person you're talking to because it hits them at an emotional level.

- To refine and improve your 30-second commercial, take a close look at each of your pain statements and create impacts for each one. Remember, impacts answer this question: "So what?" Because of X problem, what are the negative implications that follow? What happens when nobody does anything about that problem? Write down two or three negative impacts for each pain indicator.
- Then take these impact statements to your peers and your boss and start asking, "Are these the kinds of impacts that our customers are currently just living with, impacts that we can make disappear?"
- Whenever you find an impact like that, build it into your calling approach. Then practice delivering it out loud.

CHAPTER 15

Stroke, Pain, Impact

A t this point you've created your first-draft 30-second commercial, then you've added the impact for your second-draft 30-second commercial. Now let's ramp it up and find a way to really connect on a gut level with prospective buyers.

Consider the biggest obstacle to creating that kind of connection: Hubris. Pride.

It's difficult for people to admit to a total stranger that they have a challenge. You know what you're going to do to make that a little easier for them? You're going to meet them where they are. You're going to make it as easy as possible for them to engage with you and open up to you, without bruising their ego.

The strategy that does that is called *stroke, pain, impact.* That's what we'll be sharing with you in this chapter. By the way, this is advanced level sales. This is PhD stuff. It's optional and it takes some time to develop, but we do want you to see what it looks like because it's incredibly effective when it's designed and executed correctly.

> Stroke, pain, impact makes it easier
> for people to open up to you.

Terminology Check

First things first—let's define the terms. A stroke is something positive that you would say about the class of people you're working with. So for instance, if the person is a manufacturing manager, they've probably done a good job selecting the right equipment and putting together processes and schedules to deliver on time. Acknowledging that would be an example of a stroke.

Look what happens when you build in a stroke before you start talking about the pain and the impact:

You: Aryana, we do a lot of work with manufacturing managers. Often what we find is they've done a very, very good job selecting the right equipment, putting together the schedules, and designing and executing the processes that get product out on time.

That's a stroke. That points out what they're doing right. That makes it very easy for someone to raise their hand and say,

"I think this person is talking about me." After you share that stroke, you can begin to layer in the pains and the impact.

> **You (continued):** Occasionally, though, where they get frustrated is maybe they're not getting the service they need from their current manufacturer. What that means is, all of a sudden, they're not getting answers in a timely fashion. They can't get product out the door, and now they've got a dissatisfied customer. [Note the pain and the impact statements.]

Wow! When they hear that, they're locked in to your message. They want to hear more about whether you can solve this problem—because they recognize that it is, or could be, their problem.

Here's another example. In this example, notice how the first pain, which in this case was poor service, becomes the second stroke:

> **You:** Aryana, we do a lot of work with manufacturing managers. Often what we find is they've done a very, very good job selecting the right equipment, putting together the schedules, and designing and executing the processes that get product out on time. [That was the first stroke.] Maybe the service they get from the organization they chose to work with has been pretty good. [That was the second stroke.] Their challenge is that they sometimes get frustrated by back-ordered parts. Now they've got equipment sitting on the floor that can't operate. They're in downtime mode, and they're paying operators to not get any work done. That's frustrating. [Pain, impact.]

Or:

You: Aryana, we do a lot of work with manufacturing managers. Often what we find is they've done a very, very good job selecting the right equipment, putting together the schedules, and designing and executing the processes that get product out on time. [Stroke.] And they're doing a decent job even with back-ordered parts. They still meet deadlines on time. [Stroke.] However, reliability has been an issue. And so with that, they've got some unplanned downtime—and then all of a sudden they're missing their schedules. They're being called into the office of the VP of operations because now they've got customer satisfaction problems. [Pain, impact.] Have any of those things, Aryana, ever been an issue?

For a lot of people you talk to, it's going to be pretty easy to answer that question with a *yes*. That's the conversation you want. A fantastic 30-second commercial is what made it possible.

- Take your approach to the next level. Get that stroke/pain/impact cadence down, and practice it relentlessly. You may need to practice it dozens of times just to feel comfortable with the sequence. Remember, when the time comes and you actually make the call, your prospect doesn't have the script. If you miss something, no one's going to say, "Oh my gosh, you missed a stroke." So just design it, practice it until you know you feel comfortable with it, and then relax. It's not as hard as it sounds.

- Find your own voice. Find a way to make this top-level 30-second commercial structure come out as effective, authentic speech for you.

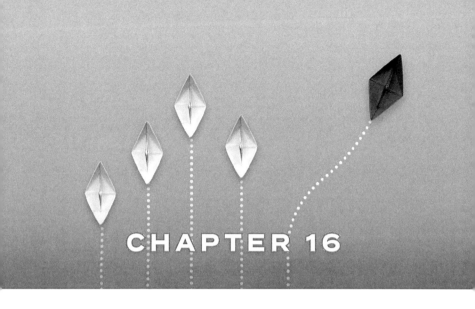

CHAPTER 16

The Wimp Junction

Let's say you're making a call using the approach you've been developing and someone bites. The other person admits they've got a challenge, and it's a challenge you can fix. What happens next?

At this point, you're reaching a critical fork in the road. On one path you can follow the traditional route and say, "Well, great. Listen, I'm going to be out in your area in the next couple of weeks. Is there a convenient time I could stop by or we could set up a Zoom call so I can tell you more?"

That's what you may be tempted to do now. Right?

The other path would be to start to dig in so you can learn a little more about the challenge they're facing.

That may seem counterintuitive to you. Is it?

That second path feels uncomfortable at first. Asking more questions and staying curious about the problem the prospect has may not be what you're used to doing. It may put butterflies in your stomach. But it's a critical moment—a moment that separates the amateurs from the professionals.

So many salespeople have reached that fork in the road where they can be traditional or they can make the choice to stand out that we've come up with a special term for it: the wimp junction.

Do the Right Thing

At the wimp junction, you've got a chance to do the right thing or you can just bail out and be traditional. In today's marketplace, you have to stand out. That means you have to face your fears, move past them, and be somewhat nontraditional.

Do not fumble the ball now that you've made it to their side of the field. Do not say, "Let's meet or set up a Zoom call." Not yet.

Why? Because you're not there yet. If you're on your way to tailgate at a football game and you see a sign that says "Stadium 25 miles ahead," you don't stop by the sign, open up the tailgate, and start the grill. You're not there yet. You've got to keep driving. It's the same way with isolating pain. Just because you see that first sign, it's doesn't mean you've gotten where you need to go.

You've got to expand the pain that you've uncovered. You've

got to get them emotionally involved before you schedule the meeting. You've got to lay the foundations for a real peer-to-peer relationship.

In this chapter, we're going to give you three simple questions that work like a charm. Your job is to practice them until they feel comfortable for you to ask when you reach this point of the discussion. That's called making the correct turn at the wimp junction. Slow it down, and you will speed up the close.

> **Slow it down to speed up a close.**

Three Questions

A word of warning: When we share these questions, a lot of people think they're so simple that they can't possibly work—and they don't use them. Don't be one of those people.

The three questions are:

1. "Can you tell me more about that?"
2. "Can you give me a specific example?"
3. "And because of that, what happened?"

So for instance, using the example of selling sales training (what we coauthors do when we're not writing books), the dialogue might go something like this:

Prospect: Our sales cycle is taking way too long.

Here, you're not going to say, "Well, I'm going to be out in your area in the next couple of weeks. Is there a convenient time we can get together?" Don't ask to set up a time for a Zoom call. Slow down.

> **You:** Help me understand that. When you say the sales cycle is taking too long, can you tell me a little bit more about that?
>
> **Prospect:** Well, when I was selling, I closed deals in four weeks. Now that I'm leading the team, it's taking people a whole lot longer than that.
>
> **You:** Can you think back and give me a real-life recent example of a sale that took too long to close, from your perspective?
>
> **Prospect [pauses, then]:** You know what? I was talking to someone on our team about this just last week, and every time I think about that deal that dragged out needlessly, I get angry. [Let them tell the story.]
>
> **You:** And because of that, what happened?
>
> **Prospect:** Well, we missed our target for the month. [That's the impact!]

Your goal with these questions is simply to get them to talk about the problem for a minute or two. They're talking themselves into your next step. People buy emotionally. They only justify their decision intellectually. Let them feel and experience the emotion.

When someone bites, relax. Don't jump like an eager puppy into, "I'm going to be in your area." Instead, ask those three questions.

Whenever someone bites on one of your pain statements, you will want to take some time to debrief after the call. Did you remember to ask these three questions? Did you wander all over the highway? Did you drive past the exit? Or did you stay focused and help them understand the impacts and examples in their world that motivate them to want to see you?

- Practice delivering your approach call, as you've currently built it, with your boss or with a colleague.
- Do some role-playing. As you role-play, be sure to ask the three questions from this chapter whenever the other person acknowledges that one of the pains you are describing is relevant in their world.
- After the role-play, debrief with your partner and ask for feedback about how you can improve your approach call.

CHAPTER 17

Set the Appointment

What's the point of all this?

Why have you been doing all that you've been doing? Why make the call in the first place? Why bother to deliver the approach you've been spending so much time tweaking and improving?

Of course, you know the answer: To get a solid, clear next step. To win a spot on the other person's calendar so you can talk in-depth about whether it makes sense to do business together. To set an appointment. That's the objective of the call.

But what kind of appointment?

Well, it might be a face-to-face, in-person appointment. It

might be a video conference with you and a single person from the buying side. It might be a video conference with a number of people involved from both sides. It might be a demo of some kind. It might be an invitation to have a follow-up phone call. It might even be spending additional time on the phone right now. The point is, you need to know what the objective is before you even start talking.

Spot the Right Exit and Take It

Be clear in advance on what your objective is for your call—and do not drive by the exit. Your goal is to close for the appointment you've identified as the aim of your call. Spot the exit and take it when it comes up.

Here are two points we often share with people about closing for the appointment.

- Closing the appointment is about directing and not asking.
- Build in some planned spontaneity.

Here's an example. They've just gone through their pains and their impacts because you asked, "Tell me more; give me an example"; "Could you be more specific?"; "Because of that, what happens?" Those questions did their job. The prospect has shared the impact with you. They're emotionally engaged. So when you have uncovered enough pain—not all the pain, mind you, but enough pain to get to the next step—you can say something like:

You: Hey, Enofe, can I make a suggestion?

Grammatically, of course, that's a question—but as a practical matter, that's a redirection of the conversation. When it's delivered properly, it sounds totally spontaneous. When you say this, it should sound like it's something you came up with on the spur of the moment, an interesting idea that just crossed your mind. But in reality, it's totally planned. It's you taking control. Once they've shared a little bit of their pain with you, they're very likely to respond positively to this request. Most of the time, the conversation will proceed as follows:

Prospect: Sure.

You: Let's do this. Take a look at your calendar. How about March 13 at eleven in the morning? Does that work for you?

Notice that those first two phrases—"Let's do this" and "Take a look at your calendar"—are authoritative instructions. They are directions, not requests. They're telling the other person what to do. That's appropriate at this stage because you're the expert in solving this kind of problem and you know what the next step should be. Your tonality should reflect that. Say these words confidently and with a sense of purpose.

An alternative that works is:

You: Hey, Enofe, can I make a suggestion?

Prospect: Sure.

You: Let's find a time to invite me out. Take a look at your calendar. March 13 at eleven in the morning. Does that work for you?

Here's another version that may work for you:

You: Hey, Enofe, can I make a suggestion?

Prospect: Sure.

You: Typically, what happens from here is that we have a chance to schedule a very brief web demo. Take a look at your calendar. March 13 at eleven in the morning. Does that work for you for a call of about 30 minutes?

Or, if your aim is to make an in-depth discussion happen right now:

You: Hey, Enofe, can I make a suggestion?

Prospect: Sure.

You: I know I may have caught you cold. It sounds like we've started a conversation we need to have in more depth. How are you on time now?

These examples are focused, purposeful, and professional. That's what needs to happen when you close for the appointment. Anything else is missing the exit.

By the way, here is what missing the exit sounds like during the call:

You: So what do you think? Does it make some sense for us to maybe get together?

That's "Mother May I" mode. Don't go there!

- Using the models in this chapter, create and practice language that closes for the appointment, that sounds spontaneous, and that commands rather than asks.
- Deliver that language until you remember it and feel comfortable saying it confidently.

CHAPTER 18

The Post-Sell: Make Sure Your Meetings Stick

Earlier, we said that your approach has the object of selling something: a mutual commitment to schedule time to talk about doing business together. When you succeed in scheduling the appointment, you close a kind of mini sale. Congratulations! Great job! Now the question is: How do you avoid having them feel buyer's remorse?

Buyer's remorse is a real thing, of course. Have you ever had people cancel meetings with you after you've set an appointment with them, or they are a no-show, or maybe you've got an appointment to have a follow-up phone conversation and they're not there at that time? So many salespeople have had these experiences. This brings us to the next step of our prospecting call, which is called the post-sell.

In fairness, sometimes salespeople don't have any of those issues. If you're one of them, maybe you can leave this step out. But if you ever have situations along those lines, think about implementing any or all of the following strategies to ensure that the meeting you just scheduled will actually happen.

Leverage the Calendar

As you are wrapping up the call, use this post-sell strategy:

> **You:** Looks like we're going to meet together on Zoom next Thursday from two to two thirty. I'll make sure that I get a calendar invite with a Zoom link over to you. In fact, better yet, maybe if you have a second to send one to me, please do.

Or even:

> **You:** Hey look, I'm not at my computer right now—are you? Any chance you could send me a calendar invite with a Zoom link?

Straightforward, simple, but very effective. This makes it their meeting, not yours. It's psychologically harder for them to cancel a meeting that they set up themselves. Try it out.

Give Them Homework

Maybe giving them homework doesn't sound like good idea. How in the world can you give a prospect homework?

Well, think about this. Recall that you're striving for equal business stature in the relationship. From that perspective, it's perfectly fine to ask the prospect to do something ahead of time. For example:

> **You:** Hey, between now and next Thursday at two, can I offer you maybe a little bit of homework, something to think about in advance so our meeting is very productive? What if you were to talk to two or three people around your office about the biggest challenges that your team is faced with and you come to our meeting with some thoughts from other people within the office about what those are?

That's giving them homework. Some people use surveys; some people use other tools to be able to ask the prospect to do a little something. The point is, having to prepare something gets more buy-in and commitment, so that when they show up, they actually have a little something that they've done—and they want to show you. As a result, they are more invested in the process than if they had done nothing at all.

Get Verbal Assurance

The third thing that you can do is just come out and ask for an assurance that you've really got the meeting. Here's what that sounds like:

You: I need to ask: Is there anything that would come up that you see on your calendar that would prevent us from getting together next Thursday at two? Any challenges or obstacles between now and then that would be a showstopper in terms of us having to reschedule or cancel? I tend to run pretty hard on my calendar, so I just want to make sure that there'd be nothing there that would prevent us from getting together.

That's your third way to post-sell the appointment and make sure that the meeting actually sticks. A lot of the people we work with opt to use all three.

- Go back and look at your calendar history over the last 30, 60, 90 days. See how many appointments you set that actually didn't stick, in which they canceled at the last minute or you had to reschedule it five times or maybe it fell through the cracks.
- If you look at the numbers and you find you're batting .950, by all means, you don't need to worry about this. You're a champion—you're doing great. Don't worry about it. But if one in five appointments actually never happens because you didn't post-sell, think about what happens if you start to implement the post-sale. You might end up with an additional sale or two every quarter as a result of the fact that more meetings are being held. How can you make the best possible use of your time?

- Once you have done that self-assessment, decide whether you need this step. If you do and you like any of the ideas we have shared with you, practice them, use them, implement them, and bring them into your system.

CHAPTER 19

The Big Up-Front Contract

Good news. You've got an appointment. You've got a *yes*. You're ready to go. You post-sold it, if that's what you needed to do. Now, the next and last step you're going to follow is known as a big up-front contract. This will clarify, for both sides, exactly what's going to happen when you do get together for the next discussion.

You'll recall that earlier on, we described a mini up-front contract that set expectations about what would happen during the call itself. This "big" one sets expectations for the next discussion, and it's important that you get it right. This agreement is going to set the stage for your next interaction, whether it's a meeting or a demo or another phone call or a video conference.

Fortunately, since you have built up some rapport with the prospect and had a meaningful conversation, you have a little time, at this point, to set a deeper up-front contract than the one you set in the first few seconds of your call. One element you're going to agree on is how much time you're going to spend with this person when you do get together. Another element to build in is asking them what they're going to want you to cover during the discussion and then sharing what you're going to want to cover. Lastly, and maybe most importantly, you want clarity about how this meeting ends. What are the possible outcomes?

What It Sounds Like

Here's an example of what the big up-front contract sounds like during a prospecting discussion:

> **You:** It sounds like we're going to meet via Zoom next Thursday at two, I've got us on the calendar for 45 minutes, and we're going to talk about X, Y, and Z when we get together. Anything else I should make sure we put in there?

> **Prospect:** No, that covers it.

> **You:** OK, great. Then, ultimately, when we're wrapping up the meeting, I think we should be able to figure out one of two things. One is if there's really not a fit for us going forward, I need you to know that's OK. But the flip side is maybe there are some next steps

we need to take. Maybe we decide to do a little bit of business together. If that's the case, let's figure that out as well. Fair?

Your goal here is to set what the next step is going to be and to do that in advance of getting together. That way, there's no mutual mystification at the end of that next all-important meeting. This is a great strategy, especially for people who are inside salespeople and who are setting appointments for other people. Make sure you do a great job of setting the up-front contract for what's going to happen, how much time it's going to take, and what the outcome of that meeting is going to be. It's a critical step in the process.

 DO THIS

- Now that you have the steps all lined up, your home-work for this chapter is simply to go back and string it all together. If you're writing everything out or you're putting it into a document, go create the outline—the full outline, by copying, pasting, and putting it all together—so that you've got one straightforward approach from beginning to end. This is your roadmap for running a really effective prospecting and approach call.

Deliver the Whole Approach, Out Loud

If you've been doing everything we've been asking you to do up to this point, you've got a detailed, advanced, refined, beginning-to-end map for your prospecting approach. Compare what you've got to the following. Your version doesn't have to match up with this exactly, of course, but it should match up fairly closely and should hit all of the major elements.

> Compare what you've done so far with
> what you see in this chapter.

The Whole Approach

[Ring, ring.]

Prospect: Juan Condita.

You [pattern interrupt and mini-up-front contract]: Hi Juan. It's Sanaz Reynolds with Dairy Deliveries. Listen, I need some help. I'm not sure if we even need to have a conversation today. Would it be OK if I briefly explain why I'm calling and then you decide whether we should continue the conversation? Is that fair?

Prospect: Sure. What's up?

You [transition into 30-second commercial]: We are a specialty equipment manufacturing company working in the dairy industry. We do a lot of work with manufacturing managers. **[Stroke:]** Often what we find is that they've done a very, very good job selecting the right equipment, putting together the schedules, and designing and executing the processes that get product out on time. **[Stroke:]** And they're doing a decent job with back-ordered parts. They get them in on time. **[Pain, impact:]** However, reliability's been an issue. And so with that, they've got some unplanned downtime—and then all of a sudden they're missing their schedules. They're being called into the office of the VP of operations because now they've got customer satisfaction problems. **[Benefit:]** So basically we create systems that keep people like you from being called into that meeting. **[Hook:]** Is any of that relevant to you?

Prospect: Yeah, sure.

You [pain discussion]: Can you tell me more about that?

Prospect: [Discusses pain.]

You: Can you give me a specific example?

Prospect: [Discusses pain.]

You: And because of that, what happened?

Prospect: [Discusses pain; is now emotionally engaged.]

You: Hey, Juan, can I make a suggestion?

Prospect: Sure.

You [close for appointment]: Let's do this. Take a look at your calendar. March 13 at 11 A.M.—does that work for you for the two of us to set up a Zoom call for maybe 45 minutes so we can look at this together in a little more depth? We may have something for you; we may not. Would you be open to a conversation?

Prospect: OK. That's fine. Yes, talk then.

You [post-sell]: Great. March 13 at 11 A.M. I'll make sure that I get a calendar invite over to you. In fact, better yet, maybe if you want, you can send it to me. Can you do that?

Prospect: Sure. Hang on. What's your email address? [You give it.] OK, just sent it.

You [give homework]: Great, got it. Hey, between now

and then, can I offer you maybe a little bit of home-work, something to think about in advance so our meeting is more productive?

Prospect: Sure.

You: What if you were to talk to two or three people around your facility about the biggest challenges that you guys are faced with in this area, and you come to our meeting with some thoughts from other people about what those are?

Prospect: Yeah, I can do that.

You [get verbal assurance]: And listen, just a couple more things before we hang up. Can you think of anything that will come up between now and the thirteenth that could cause you to change or cancel the appointment?

Prospect: No. I'll be there.

You [big up-front contract, Part 1]: All right. It sounds like we're going to meet on March 13 at 11 A.M., I've got us on the calendar for 45 minutes, and we're go-ing to talk about X, Y, and Z when we get together. Anything else I should make sure we put in there?

Prospect: No, that covers it.

You [big up-front contract, Part 2]: OK, great. Then before I let you go, let's preview our outcomes on this very briefly. Ultimately, when we're wrapping up that meeting, I think we should be able to figure out one of two things. One is if there's really not a fit for us going forward, I need you to know that's OK. You can tell me that. But the flip side is that maybe there are some next steps we need to take. Maybe down the road we decide to do a little bit of business together. If that's the case, let's figure that out as well. Fair?

Prospect: Sounds good to me.

- Compare your written approach to ours. Make sure you're not missing anything.
- Once you're positive that you've got everything in the right place and that it sounds right coming out of your mouth, say it out loud a dozen times.
- Record at least three of those times.
- Share one of the recordings with a colleague or with your boss, and ask for a critique. What could you improve in terms of tonality? Pacing? Authenticity?
- Is there any content that needs tweaking? If so, tweak it.

CHAPTER 21

Generating Introductions When You Didn't Get an Appointment

Every prospecting interaction pays dividends. Every single one.

What do we mean by that? Even if you get a *no*, you can learn something and improve. And, even if you get a *no*, you can ask yourself where the potential is—and pursue that.

Ready to Get Uncomfortable?

Right now, we're going to share something with you that may make you a little bit uncomfortable. It ties back to that critical priority we shared with you in Chapter 3 about generating warm leads rather than relying on cold leads.

What we're going to share with you now made us uncomfortable the first time we tried it. It's not so much the activity itself but the timing. Right after you hear a *no* in a prospecting discussion, that's the time you can actually ask for an introduction. Believe us, this can dramatically increase the number of introductions you generate.

> Dramatically increase the number of introductions you generate by asking for them when you get a *no*.

It sounds wild, right?

Way back when, as coauthor of this book John was starting out as a sales trainer, David Sandler (his mentor) told him, "John, I want you to get 10 appointments a week."

John said, "Got it. David—but what do I do to make that happen?"

He said, "Make 150 dials a week, set 10 appointments."

This was over 25 years ago, so that formula made sense. John's first week he made 150 dials, talked to 50 people, and got zero appointments. He couldn't even do the math about how badly he was doing, but he knew he wasn't headed in the right direction. He went back to David Sandler and asked for some coaching.

Sandler said, "Well, John, are you asking for any introductions once you get a *no?*"

"Of course not, David. No one is going to give me an introduction if they've never spoken to me before. Why in the world would they do that?"

"Are you saying that because you have asked in the past and you know that no one has ever given you an introduction—or because you just know?"

"David, I just know."

"Let me ask you something, John. Are you competitive?"

"Sure, I'm competitive."

"OK, prove me wrong. Over the next three weeks, can you ask for an introduction once you get a *no?*"

"Sure, but it's not going to work. What's my language?"

Sandler gave John the language that we are going to share with you now. John said it out loud 25 times and then used that language. And on the very first call, the woman he reached gave him three introductions! John didn't even have to believe it was going to work.

To this day, John remembers the name of the woman he reached that day. It was Helen Alex. She was listed first in a Chamber of Commerce directory; that's why she got John's first call. Here's what it sounded like for him—and what it could sound like for you, every time you get a *no:*

> **You:** Hey, listen, it doesn't sound like I can help you right now, but I appreciate your time. Maybe you could help me. If you were me in my industry, would you have any recommendations of people in your network, in your circle, who you think would be open to

having a similar conversation to the one we just had?

Helen, who had just taken a pass on the chance to meet with John, heard that, went silent for a moment, and said, "I can't think of anybody."

And John, realizing he was at another wimp junction, heard himself saying, "Well, Helen, maybe it's a partner company. Maybe it's one of your suppliers, maybe it's one of your customers."

Helen said, "I only have three customers."

John said, "OK, who do you deal with?"

And she gave John the names of the presidents of three different engineering companies.

John said, "Do you mind if I reach out to them? And tell them we talked?"

"Knock yourself out."

When he hung up the phone, John was shocked. He called David Sandler, explained what had just happened, and said, "Now what?" He felt like he had just caught a bear but didn't know what to do about it.

Sandler said, "Don't squander your leverage." And he told John what to say. Do you remember? We've already shared it with you, but just in case you've forgotten, here it is again:

> **You:** I just had the chance to talk to Helen. She thought it might be important we speak, and I promised I would call.

Two of the three engineering companies John called did not go anywhere. But guess what? The first president he called said, "You know what? Your timing is great."

They became John's very first client. They introduced him to a sister client, who then introduced him to a very large multinational industrial company, who then introduced him to an executive search company, who then introduced him to another industrial company, who then introduced him to a Fortune 100 company. The moral of the story is that millions of dollars of revenue came from that call he made to Helen Alex and from being gutsy enough and well-trained enough to ask for that introduction even after the *no*.

Think about that for a moment.

Will you implement this now? You certainly have nothing to lose.

> You can't lose what you don't have.

Think about the last 10 calls you made. How many times, if you did get a *no*, did you ask for an introduction? If the answer is zero, you're not alone. It's time to change. You may not believe anybody will give you any introductions, and we felt the same way. But you need to know that for us and for the people we train, the number of positive responses is approximately one out of five. Why would you walk away from that?

- Practice and deliver the technique we shared with you in this chapter.

CHAPTER 22

The 5 Rules of Prospecting Behavior

At the beginning of the book, you'll recall that we talked about the Success Triangle. Once again, that's attitude (your beliefs and your self-concept), technique (knowing how to do what you need to do), and behavior (actually doing what you need to do). We've spent a whole lot of time on technique in the previous chapters. Now it's time to do a deeper dive on one of the other corners of the Success Triangle: behavior.

The idea here is that once you have proficiency in the core technique of discussing what you do with prospects and setting the meeting, something cool happens. The act of executing on that technique, as part of a well-thought-out prospecting plan, and simply doing the behaviors will improve your competencies and your self-concept.

> ### Do the behaviors!

In our experience, doing the behaviors is often the key to lifting up the other two corners of the Success Triangle. Now, we haven't given you everything there is to know yet about improving your mindset; we'll look at that in-depth a little later on in the book. And we certainly haven't shared every relevant technique with you yet; there's more about digital prospecting to be found in Chapter 31. But if you've followed us this far and you've done everything we've asked you to do, you've now got the foundation laid in. It's time to start building on that by setting up and executing your prospecting plan.

The 5 Rules of Prospecting Behavior

So let's drill into some basic rules about prospecting behaviors that will empower you to create and implement a rock-solid prospecting plan. There are five in particular that we want to share with you. Follow these rules as you go forward, and you will be more likely to lift up all three corners of the Success Triangle.

Rule 1: Never manage your numbers—manage your behavior.

What this means is that if you ever fall into the trap of imagining that you can manage your sales outcomes, you need to do a little bit of a reality check. The truth is, you can't control that. There's no magic wand you can wave that will make someone decide to buy. What you can control is what you do. How many conversations do you initiate? How many new contacts do you make? How many introductions do you ask for? Whether people decide to buy from you is interesting, of course, but the closing numbers are what's known as a lagging indicator. What you are interested in are the leading indicators, the behaviors that lead up to the point where people decide to buy from you. Those behaviors are entirely in your control.

Rule 2: You can't manage what you can't control.

This is a corollary of Rule 1, of course, but it's worth examining on its own. If you can't control something, it follows logically that it doesn't make a whole lot of sense to invest major amounts of time, attention, energy, or worry trying to affect that thing you can't control. If you're spending all or even a significant chunk of your time working on things that you don't necessarily control (like whether someone likes you or feels good about you or decides to buy from you), that's a problem, and you need to change course.

Rule 3: You don't have to like prospecting—you just have to do it.

If you spend time with the most successful people you know, one of the things that you're going to notice is that a lot of times they don't like things that they do, but they take action and execute on the behavior anyway. With apologies to Nike, they just do it. That's a decision. As a result of that decision to stop fixating on whether or not they like something that's within their control, something that they know they need to take action on, and instead to just do it, they are successful. When you learn to act in spite of how you feel, you're going to be more successful and you're going to get more business done. The most successful people act in spite of how they feel.

> The most successful people in life take
> action in spite of how they feel.

This isn't just a secret to massive success at prospecting—it's a secret to massive success in life. Just do it!

Rule 4: You can't fail at prospecting. You can only fail to prospect.

When we talk to people about the behavior part of the Success Triangle, in most cases, we find that they rate themselves the lowest on the behavior corner—meaning they know what they should be doing, but they're not doing it. They're letting that attitude corner control the behavior corner. So we need to remind them that they really can't fail at prospecting. If you know what to do—and you do now—it's just a question of whether or not you're going to execute consistently and then track the results.

Rule 5: Every unsuccessful discussion yields compound interest.

You may make a call on Monday and find that actually nothing comes from it until Wednesday, Thursday, Friday,

Saturday, or the following week—or even later. (Remember John's experience with Helen Alex?) One way that you can earn compound interest on calls that don't get you an appointment right away is that good outcomes can still happen down the line. Those wouldn't have happened without you taking action. But you know what else? You also learn important things from a call that doesn't produce an appointment or a meeting. You can look for areas where you can improve your tonality, your delivery, and your approach.

Forget about "always be closing." That's nonsense. You can, however, always be learning. When you do enough behaviors and generate enough activity, you will benefit from both kinds of compound interest. Rule 5 reminds you to keep at it.

- Write down the five prospecting behavior rules and post them where you can see them every day.

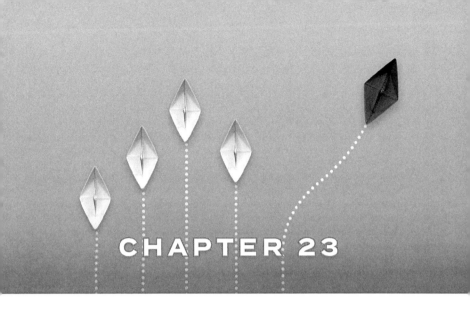

CHAPTER 23

The Cookbook Creator

When you follow a recipe in a cookbook for, say, a chocolate cake, you assume it's been tested, right? You assume that there has been some kind of quality check along the way. You assume that if you carefully follow all the steps in the precise order the recipe lays out for you, using all the same ingredients, the end result is going to be a great chocolate cake.

You may not have thought of this as a metaphor for success in sales, but it is. The recipe is your behavioral plan. And the chocolate cake is you, hitting your financial and personal goals.

What is the recipe you're following to make success happen? How carefully has that recipe been tested? Does it work?

Perhaps most importantly, when are you going to get your chocolate cake?

When you think about your behaviors and activities and how those show up in your plan, one of the big questions to ask is:

- "How many introductions, how many conversations, how many meetings, and ultimately how many sales do I need to have in order to hit my numbers and to meet my financial goals each month?"

To help you answer that question, we've given you a tool called the Cookbook Creator (based on Sandler's Cookbook for Success). It shows up in the Appendix. This tool allows you to generate a recipe for financial success in your business. It helps you isolate exactly how many appointments, how many meetings, and how many sales you need to back into your own personal financial goals—and what the specific behaviors are that generate the outcome you want.

Your job, once you finish reading this chapter, is to go to the Appendix and take a deep dive into the Cookbook Creator.

This tool will ask you to formalize your monthly financial goal. What do you want to bring in? How much is going to come in the form of salary? How much is going to come in the form of commission? How many sales do you need each month? What are the specific behaviors—the leading indicators, the stuff you can count—that will reliably generate that number of sales?

Now, here's our prediction about what's going to happen when you start this. As you're working with this tool, you're going to say to yourself, "Well, I don't know how many initial introductions or meetings it takes; I don't know how many presentations it takes; I don't know what my average sale is."

News flash: This is what we call head trash.

It's the result of a self-concept that isn't serving you: a dysfunctional mindset, a way of thinking about yourself and your market that you've grown used to, or a way of looking at the world that you're familiar with but that is not helping you. "I don't know" is a justification for the status quo. If you are going to just do it, which is the bottom line of Rule 3 in the previous chapter, you're going to move past that justification. Your job now is take a little time and figure out the ratios to the best of your ability.

There is a lot more to say about attitude, which, as you will recall, is a corner on the Success Triangle. For now, we're just going to give you some coaching you can use. Every time you hear yourself say or think, "I don't know," just add the word "yet." You don't know yet. But you're going to find out. Then, find out. You do have an average. Everybody has an average. We realize you might have some big sales and some small ones, some sales that take a while and some sales that happen more rapidly, but it's your job now to get the best information you can, from whatever source you can, about your personal average. Throw out the head trash. Move beyond your comfort zone. Just do it.

If you find it takes you 10 presentations to get one close, then you're going to need to run the math so that you can back into how many initial discussions you need to have in order to get one contact, which leads to one first meeting, which leads to presentations, which leads to sales. You're going to need to break down the specific prospecting activities you did to have those initial discussions. Were they making phone calls, doing email outreach (there are some cool ideas on email outreach waiting for you in Chapter 31), asking for and giving introductions, sharing leads with folks who call on the same type of people you call on, attending networking events, giving talks to groups and associations, or something else? What are the handful of prospecting activities that resonate well with you, that you believe you can succeed in, that you'll make a commitment to being the best in? Map those to your cookbook and find a way to build them into your prospecting plan.

What you're really doing with this exercise is backing your way into unearthing the number of initial conversations you need to generate on a daily basis. At the end of each week, you'll know for sure whether you're on track for meeting your numbers, and you can adjust accordingly if you're not. By the time you get done with the Cookbook Creator, you'll know exactly what your minimum daily behavior target is. Remember, those daily behaviors are the only things you can control.

- Go to the Appendix right now and spend at least 30 minutes working your way through the Cookbook Creator. Identify your personal daily behavioral targets. These should match up with your goals and your preferences in terms of behaviors—not anyone else's.*

---

* When you go through the Cookbook Creator, you will notice that it asks you how many sales you need per month. If your business has a longer sales cycle and you close only a few deals a year, make the adjustment necessary to have the tool fit your business. The concepts are the same regardless of the sales cycle.

Tracking the Numbers

You've got your prospecting plan in place. You know what your activities are. Now it's time to do some tracking. How are you going to make sure that you stay on track?

There's more than one way to go about this, and there's no one right way. You've got to find what works for you. Some companies are going to have a CRM system already in place, and it's going to do some tracking for you. That can work well, but there are some limitations to that. For instance, if you're going to networking events and you want to track that, that may not be an easy thing to put into your CRM. You may need to come up with an additional system on your own. Sometimes your company is going to tell you what you need to do, and that's fine. Do what you need to do in that situation.

You can always set up and update a personalized spreadsheet or data entry program that enables you to track everything you need to track, assuming you feel comfortable with that kind of setup work. Of course, if you don't, there's the old-school option: paper and pen or pencil. It's definitely better than not tracking your activity, and for some people, it's what they're most comfortable with. You can use a notebook or a bunch of index cards—whatever works for you. If you've ever seen a movie where someone is in prison and keeps track of their days by scratching lines onto the wall, that's pretty much the system we're talking about. It's not particularly high-tech, but hey, if it works, it works. Sometimes, for some people, the simplest idea is the best when it comes to keeping track of activity and behavior.

Get Social

Another recommendation is for you to have an accountability partner you can discuss your behavior targets with on an ongoing basis. This is someone you meet with weekly to review what you each said you were going to do and what you each actually did in terms of prospecting activity. This takes about 15 minutes.

> Find an accountability partner.

If you can make the commitment to do this with someone you trust and whose opinion you care about, you will find that this social connection can deliver a powerful incentive for each of you to just do it.

- Decide how you will be tracking your activity numbers.
- Set up weekly meetings with an accountability partner.

CHAPTER 25

Time Blocking

S o here's the challenge. How do you make sure those prospecting activities from your cookbook actually get done?

Before you say, "Well, I'll just put a reminder in my calendar," consider that a lot of people have an entry in their Outlook or Google calendar that reads "Make prospecting calls"—and that reminder can be more than a decade old! So maybe using the calendar in the way they're using it right now is not the answer.

One of our favorite Sandler rules is, "You can never fail at prospecting—unless you fail to prospect." That's a point you want to bear in mind here. How do you make it harder to fail to prospect in the first place?

> You can never fail at prospecting—
> unless you fail to prospect.

Yes, you may have the best of intentions. But since prospecting is strategically vital but not necessarily urgent, any reminders often get ignored. That's the reality. The goal has to be to change what you're doing and to change it in such a way that the urgent stuff still gets done and the behavior that gets entered into your tracking system increases over time—and meets your targets. What can you do to move the needle?

The answer is, you've got to start thinking differently about the way you use your time. One of the concepts we want to strongly suggest is called *time blocking*.

Set the Appointment

Time blocking means not just reminding yourself to prospect but setting an appointment with yourself to prospect—and then keeping that appointment.

You've got to start thinking of doing your daily prospecting behaviors as paying yourself first. In other words, as sales professionals, accept and embrace the reality that prospecting is your #1 scheduling priority. Prospecting gets scheduled first.

Let's say you work a 40-hour week, and let's say you figure out, based on the daily behaviors you identified in your cookbook, that you need to prospect for six of those hours. What does that mean in terms of time blocking? It means you start your scheduling, every single week, by acknowledging that you don't really have 40 hours to schedule. You actually have 34 because those six prospecting hours are already spoken for. Set up those six hours in the calendar before you set up anything else. Not only that—also color-code them, so you can see at a glance exactly where they fall, and defend those prospecting slots on your calendar vigorously.

Are emergencies going to come up from time to time? Sure. Are you going to be flexible about those emergencies? Of course. Are you going to accept anything less than six hours a week (or whatever the number is) in terms of color-coded, scheduled prospecting time? Absolutely not!

Think about your single best customer, your single best client, or your best prospect. Take a moment now to visualize that person. If you had an appointment scheduled with that individual, would you just cancel it the minute something else came up?

We hope not!

But guess what? Right now (if you're like most of the people we coach through the time blocking process), you're canceling appointments with yourself. And you're even more important to your business than that client or prospect.

You need to have that same level of commitment. When you put those time blocks in your calendar, commit to keeping them. Why? Because you are the most important person in your territory. You're the one who needs to be proactive and to find ways to make things work. That means you've got to stick to your time blocks.

- Take a look at your cookbook and all your prospecting activities, and translate them into a realistic weekly time commitment that can be expressed in hours. (Only you can figure out what this number is. Make sure it is enough to execute on all of the behaviors you have identified.)
- Then, put time blocks next to them. If networking is part of your strategy, how much time does that take on a weekly basis? Break it down; budget the time. If making warm calls or cold calls is part of your strategy, how much time do you plan to spend on that to meet your cookbook goals? If having lunch with someone you can trade leads with is one of your key strategies, what does that look like, broken down into a weekly time allotment?
- Add it all up, then take the time blocks and put them into your calendar, color-coded. Don't put in a six-hour time block and try to work it all at once. Ideally, you will identify a number of two- or four-hour time blocks you can schedule—and defend. Do this before you schedule anything else for the week. Give your prospecting time blocks the priority.
- Make sure this schedule fits your style. Make sure it's something you will feel comfortable doing.
- Then (and this is vitally important), tell your accountability partner about what you've scheduled and when you've scheduled it. Ask them to hold you accountable to do the things that you have committed to doing.

CHAPTER 26

Research

L et's talk for just a moment about the research you need to do in order for you to prospect effectively.

It is quite likely that you will have to do research for at least some of your prospect outreach. The good news is that you live in a world where it is fairly easy to find out (for instance) whether someone is on LinkedIn, knows one of your contacts on LinkedIn, or has written an article or given a speech recently. Yes, leveraging information from LinkedIn is important; identifying potential introduction sources is important; and tracking down speeches and articles you can reference and mention during conversations is potentially important too.

The big question is, when should tracking down that kind of stuff happen?

If you're not careful, you can spend a whole lot of time doing research that is definitely relevant but that isn't prospecting. Think about your calendar and the time you have now set aside to do prospecting. At that time, you definitely want to be prospecting, not researching.

Where does the word "prospecting" even come from? From the California Gold Rush, back in the 19th century. Prospectors were the people who actively went out searching for gold in a variety of ways. When they were digging, they were prospecting. When they were swinging a pickaxe, they were prospecting. When they were swishing river water and rocks around in that specially designed pan, scanning the rocks for glints of gold, they were prospecting. But here's the big question: When they were researching what kind of shovel or pickaxe felt best in their hands, figuring out what kind of pan to buy, or buying and studying maps to get a clearer idea of the next river they wanted to check out, were they prospecting?

No! Those activities—getting the right equipment, securing the right map—were important. They had to happen at some point. But prospectors knew full well that they weren't going to get paid for those activities. As a result, they didn't spend all day doing those activities.

Think of the hours you've set aside for prospecting as pay-time. Why? Because your prospecting behaviors, by definition, connect in a measurable way to revenue generation. Think of the time you need for research as no-pay-time. Why? Because you could research for hours, days, weeks, months, or years, and at the end of all that time you spent doing nothing but researching, you would have lots and lots of information but no dollars.

> Schedule research time separately. Don't research during scheduled prospecting time. Save that for no-pay-time.

Pay-time is time spent in front of or speaking with a customer or prospect. No-pay-time activities (like research) need to be scheduled for outside the time you have blocked off for prospecting.

Side note: Often we find people are spending way too much time doing the research before they reach out. A little bit is OK, but if you find yourself doing a whole lot of research to prepare for each and every outreach, you might want to ask yourself, "Am I doing creative avoidance? Am I actually experiencing some call reluctance and I'm just calling it research?"

Did your prospect recently write a white paper or give a presentation or get a promotion? Cool! You definitely do want to know about that kind of thing, and yes, you want to be in a position to mention what you've learned at some appropriate moment.

But.

You probably don't want to spend eight hours tracking down information about someone who isn't doing business with you and who hasn't yet shown any interest in doing so. Yes, you want to know when the white paper came out and what the topic is, but let's face it, you don't have time to read all 40 pages. Yes, you want to know the title of the presentation the person delivered, but it probably doesn't make sense to invest 90 minutes watching it on YouTube. Yes, you want to know, broadly speaking, what this person is responsible for in their new position, but you don't need to memorize their company org chart.

Bottom line: It is your responsibility to do the research you need to do to make a personal, unexpected, and significant connection—but it is also your responsibility to reduce the amount of time it takes to do the research that will enable you to make that connection. Your goal should be to identify two or three cool points of interest about a given contact, not to write the definitive 5,000-word Wikipedia entry for that person. This means instilling a sense of time discipline, and it means learning to use the tools at your disposal more effectively.

One best practice we strongly recommend is to do the research necessary for two or three people you plan to reach out to and finding out just two or three cool things about each—without using up any of the time in the time blocks you've scheduled for prospecting. Another is to give yourself a specific list of people you are committing to contact during those periods you have blocked off exclusively for prospecting. If you make that list and then share it with your accountability partner, you will be motivated to do your research during other time slots and to spend your pay-time on outreach.

By the way, the LinkedIn Levers tool, which you will find in the Appendix, will help you use your research time more efficiently for each person who shows up on your list. So will this Google link (www.google.com/advanced_search), which allows you to search for a given name whenever it shows up in PDF format. This can be helpful when it comes to quickly tracking down white papers, presentation agendas, and other interesting bits of background information on someone you are planning to contact.

- Look closely at the time you have blocked off for prospecting. If you haven't already done so, make sure that you have a compiled list of specific people you need to reach out to during that scheduled time.
- When the time comes, follow through on the commitment to use pay-time to your benefit. Save the research for no-pay-time. Once you have time blocked in your calendar to prospect, use that time to look for business—not on researching to find people to speak with.

CHAPTER 27

Gumball Prospecting

A lot of times when salespeople make prospecting calls, especially if it's an introduction or an inbound lead, they feel a lot of pressure to convince the prospect that they should agree to whatever the next step in the salesperson's process is. The salesperson feels like it's their job to get the prospect to do whatever they want them to do, when they want them to do it.

Here is a true story from coauthor Mark's childhood that may help to take some of the pressure off trying to convince someone they should work with you.

When Mark was a kid, his folks used to take him to a store that had a really big gumball machine. It had the big glass ball on the outside, and you could see all the colors of the gumballs inside. He always wanted one of the green gumballs. To this day, he's not sure why he was so fixated on getting a green one, but for him, that was perfection. A green gumball, for Mark, was the best you could get.

Every week, when his parents would take him to the store, he'd go up to the machine, put the quarter in the slot, and turn the handle. The thing that made this exciting was that you never knew what color gumball you were going to get. As that machine made its rumbling sound and you could hear the gumball hit the little metal door, there would be all this wonderful anticipation.

Mark would open up the little door to find out. Some weeks, out would come a red gumball, or blue, or yellow. Mark would think, "I didn't want that. I wanted green."

Even back when he was a kid, Mark knew that there was no way he could stare at a red gumball and turn it into a green one. It can't be done. The gumball color is what it is. The best thing you can do as a kid who wanted a green gumball and didn't get one is put in another coin and try again. Sooner or later, you're going to get green.

Years later, Mark was working with some clients, trying to convince them to work with him on a project, and the conversation just wasn't going where Mark wanted it to go. And at that moment, for some reason, it hit him: He was looking at a red gumball! These people weren't going to buy—they just didn't get it. Nothing Mark was going to say or do was going to change the situation. It was time to accept that these people had disqualified themselves. It was time to move on.

> **Learn to recognize when prospects disqualify themselves.**

That moment of clarity for Mark can be a moment of clarity for you too. If you look at prospecting the same way he looked at that gumball machine, it might make it easier for you. When you reach out to someone, in effect you're putting a quarter in the slot, you're turning the handle, and a gumball is coming out. That color is going to be what it's going to be. It's either going to be something you're looking for or something you're not.

Let's say the green gumballs are people who want to talk to you further and schedule a next step; people who just want to be done with the whole interaction are the red gumballs. It's time to accept that red is red and to stop putting yourself under the stress and pressure of trying to convert that red gumball into a green one. Yes, you can influence someone by the questions you ask. By and large, though, your job when it comes to prospecting is to go out and put the coin in the slot, turn it, and see what kind of prospect you get.

Are they what you're looking for? Yes or no?

Let's face the facts. Not everybody is going to say yes.

You can try to influence them to some degree, but at the end of the day, they're going to be what they're going to be and do what they're going to do.

Sure, some people are going to say, "Hey, I'm ready to meet

with you. I'm ready to set up a demo. I'm ready to take the next step. Let's do it." But some people aren't.

A lot of people are going to say things like, "I'm happy. We're good. We don't need it." And the big question is, how will you respond to something like that?

Gumball Techniques You Can Use

Let's talk about a couple of techniques you can use when people say things like "We're good" to figure out whether you're looking at a red or a green gumball. This is important because when you think about the conditioned responses people have, you realize that sometimes people say things just to end the conversation. But there still might be an opportunity there, waiting to be uncovered. On the other hand, sometimes there's just no daylight at all. You want to know which situation you're looking at before you move on. If it's a red gumball, you definitely do want to move on. But is it? That's what you need to figure out.

Let's assume your 30-second commercial and the hook that comes at the end of it don't elicit any pain. Are you done yet? No. You need to find out: Is this a red gumball? Or maybe a green one? One way to find out is to ask an open-ended question.

Instead of saying, "Thanks for your time; have a nice day," plant your feet and ask your question. Here's what it might sound like:

Prospect: We're fine. Everything is good.

You: Look, I appreciate your bringing that up in terms of reconditioning your widgets. It sounds like you've got things under control. I'm curious: If you did think about your business in terms of widget reconditioning, what would you say your biggest challenge is?

Fill in the "widget" blank in what you just read with whatever industry language you need. The idea here is to ask the question with the biggest possible opening. You want to leave the barn door wide open and see what happens. Sometimes—not all the time, of course, but sometimes—that question will elicit a response, assuming you haven't sounded like every other salesperson on earth up to this point. That response may point you toward a conversation, and that conversation could point you toward an introduction or toward a next step. Green gumball!

There's an interesting and very effective variation on this that you may want to consider using. This variation isn't a wide-open question like the one we just shared with you. In fact, it's almost the opposite because it focuses in on a tightly defined subject. It's something Sandler calls a negative reverse.

This kind of question basically takes the other person's point of view, expands it, positions it as a fact, and then asks a question that invites them to correct it. So instead of asking, "Are you happy with the level of service you're getting?" (which, let's face it, would not open any doors for you), you are going to point that question in the opposite direction and say something like this:

> **You:** So if I'm hearing you right, it sounds like you couldn't be happier with the level of service you're getting right now—they're in touch when you need them, they're solving problems before they happen, and they're taking good care of you. Is that right?

Full disclosure: This kind of question takes practice to learn to deliver. If you do plan to use this technique, be sure to rehearse it until what you say sounds authentic, professional, and curious. (As opposed to sarcastic, which is not what you want.)

Now, when you deliver the negative reverse properly, there will be some discussions—not all, but some—where you hear this:

Prospect: Actually, I do feel like the support has slipped over the last couple of months.

That's the sound of them now wanting to open up the door. That's the sound of them waiting for you to ask more questions. That's the sound of a conversation that's ready for you to move it forward. And maybe, just maybe, that's the sound of a green gumball.

With both of these techniques, it's important to remember that you are not trying to push your way in the door. You're just turning the handle and seeing what kind of gumball you get.

 DO THIS

- Take the pressure off yourself. Stop trying to change people. Remember that the only pressure you should feel is the pressure to qualify the opportunity in the right way. That means asking yourself: "Is this what I'm looking for? Yes or no?"
- Practice one or both of the techniques for handling the "We're all set/we're happy" response from prospects. Write down what you plan to say, then say it out loud until these techniques feel comfortable to you.

CHAPTER 28

Gumball Prospecting, Continued

In this chapter, we want to share some best "gumball prospecting" practices you can use when you find yourself faced with two very common scenarios: someone who tells you they have no time and someone who tells you they're all set—that they are already working with someone, that they already have a solution to the problem, or that they're already doing something that they don't feel like changing.

No matter how strong your approach, no matter how much

you've practiced, no matter how much role-playing you've done, there are going to be people who say these things to you. When people tell you it's a bad time or they're all set, your job is to figure out: Is this a red gumball or a green one? What should that conversation look and sound like? The dialogues below will give you some ideas.

Handling "This Is a Bad Time"

Let's look first at the person who tells you that you've called at a bad time.

That could be a red gumball or a green one. You just don't know yet. Here's a very simple way you can find out, working from a pattern interrupt that you use to start the call:

Prospect: Actually, this is a terrible time. I just can't talk right now.

You: OK, no worries. Would it be helpful if I took simply 30 seconds to tell you the reason? This way we can figure out if we even need the call.

Prospect: Yeah, I guess so. Go ahead.

And you're into the mini up-front contract. You've got a chance to start a conversation.

Our experience is that salespeople tend to overreact a little bit when they hear, "This is a bad time." More often than you may imagine, people will agree to the 30-second summary because they are willing to make that trade-off just to find out what the call is about.

Handling "We're Happy Now"

Now let's look at the conversation where the person tells you they're all set, they're happy with what they have. Here's how that conversation might go:

Prospect: Danica, I've got to tell you. I'm pretty happy with who I'm using now.

You: Hey listen, no worries, Orrin. I appreciate your time. It's one of the reasons why I reached out. I wasn't sure… who are you using now as your plumbing distributor?

Prospect: We use Smooth Plumbing.

You: Got it. And what do you like about them?

Prospect: Well, I've known them for a long time. They're good guys. They show up when we ask them to.

You: Yeah, fair enough. No, again, I appreciate it. Hey, no one is perfect, true, Orrin?

Prospect: Yeah, I guess not.

You: If you can pick even one small thing you think Smooth might be able to do differently or better, and I'm not saying X, Y, Z is the answer, but if you had to pick even one small thing you think they could do differently or better, what would it be?

Prospect: Well, it's kind of hard to say. We had been looking for local distribution—local parts to increase accessibility. It's kind of one thing we're working on with them right now.

You: So when you say increased parts for local accessibility, help me understand that. Can you tell me a little bit more about that?

Prospect: Well, I think our ability to get parts quickly is important. Every now and then they've been out of stock or they haven't had something at their warehouse. So we'd like to have some stuff that's actually on-site for us—more parts available to us. We're still working on that.

Now you've got a pain indicator, and now you get a chance to expand on that pain.

You: Can you give me a real-life example, Orrin? [Prospect shares an example.] And because of that, what happens?

And the conversation moves forward from there. Where there is a pain, there is a discussion. Where there is a discussion, there's the chance for a next step.

Here's another dialogue example you can use as a model in this situation:

Prospect: Yeah, Terri, thanks for the call, but I'm really happy with my current broker.

You: Yeah, no worries, Jim. Again, I appreciate the time. It's one of the reasons why I reached out. Who are you using today?

Prospect: Long-Term Help.

You: OK, and what do you like about them?

Prospect: They show up. They take me to lunch.

You: Yeah. Well, that's nice.

Prospect: Seriously, though, they're good people.

You: Jim, no one is perfect, though. Fair?

Prospect: Yeah. That's fair.

You: If Long-Term could even do one small thing differently or better, and I'm not saying we have the answer if it's X,Y, or Z, what do you think that would be?

Prospect: Yeah, I don't know. Again, I just think they do a really good job.

Would you be tempted to end the call here? A lot of salespeople would. But there are a lot of things you can still do to turn the handle and see what kind of gumball you're looking at. For instance, you can set up a question based on something your company does that you are pretty sure the competition does not do. This particular technique is called an assumptive question. Watch how it works:

You: Yeah. Well, listen, Jim, I appreciate your time. It sounds like you are all set. Let me ask you this. When your current broker comes in on a quarterly basis to run those small group meetings to get a lot of the questions answered about the new benefit plans, so they don't always have to end up running to your desk, and taking your time, how are those meetings going? Are they pretty well attended? Is there a lot of interaction?

Prospect: Yeah, I'm not sure I understand. We're not doing that today.

You: Jim, I guess I'm not so sure I understand. I suppose my question was, when your current broker comes in to facilitate these quarterly small group meetings with your employees, answering a lot of the questions that typically might end up on your desk, I guess my question was more like...

Prospect: You mean getting everybody together?

You: Yeah.

Prospect: All the employees?

You: Right. My question was how are your people responding to that? What are the interactions like?

Prospect: Well, I mean, we're not doing that today.

You: Is that something you told them you didn't want?

Prospect: No. Actually, you're making me think that might save some time because our HR people are constantly being bombarded by the same questions.

You: Do you think there's any value in that?

Prospect: There could be.

You: And tell me why. What's your thinking behind that one?

Prospect: Well, our HR manager, Ebony, has complained a couple of times, and rightly so, that she's getting the same questions over and over and over regarding benefits.

You: OK. So I'm trying to see the world through your eyes. When you say she's complained about something, if it's even possible, can you think back and maybe even give me a recent example?

Prospect: Well, we were at a staff meeting the other day, and she was just saying she's out of time...

You: OK.

Prospect: And we were saying, "Well, what's clogging up your schedule?" She said, "Well, I do get a lot of questions about benefits, and they're kind of the same questions over and over."

You: Yeah.

Prospect: I don't know if we really derived an action out of that, per se. But it was brought up.

You: What do you think would happen if she had the time? What would she be working on?

Prospect: Well, we're not hiring as fast as we should be, that's for sure.

You: Can I make a suggestion?

Prospect: Sure.

And from there you move on to the appointment close.

Again, what you just read was a fairly sophisticated technique using assumptive questions. Notice what happened: You made an assumption about the great things that they do at the organization (in this case, running quarterly meetings) with the internal hope and expectation that the competition doesn't do that particular thing. Sometimes, when you turn that handle, you'll get a green gumball. Does it always work? Of course not. Will it generate some appointments for you? Definitely.

- Write down and role-play the strategies you learned in this chapter for dealing with the "Bad time" and "We're happy" responses.

CHAPTER 29

Voicemail

"**Y**ou've reached my voicemail. Please leave a message, and I will get back to you just as soon as possible. [Beep.]"

Now what do you do?

You know you're not going to have a 100% connection rate when you're prospecting. You know you're going to get voicemails. So now it's the age-old question: to leave a message or not to leave a message?

The hard truth is, in this period following a global pandemic, very few voicemail messages are getting returned. That's not the way it was a few years ago, but it is the way things are now. In today's environment, here's what we tell our clients to do:

155

1. Do leave a message, but keep the message as short as possible: name, company, phone number, and repeat the phone number for clarity. Don't leave any other information. The obvious exception to this is a voicemail you leave for someone to whom a client or ally has introduced you, which should sound something like this:

You: Hi, Rusty, Lieu Sanchez of Financial Wizards here. I was speaking with Yolanda Brown, and she thought it might be important for us to speak. I promised her I would give you a call. My number is 555-555-1212. Again, that's Lieu Sanchez, 555-555-1212.

2. Be sure to speak clearly. Often, your message will be automatically transcribed. Assume the person will be reading what you say. Make it easy for the automated system to translate your message.

3. Last but not least, consider following up with a parallel email or text message on the same day that you leave your voicemail message. Think of this as a one-two punch. You want to try to reach people through a variety of different platforms. (You will read more about the one-two punch concept in Chapter 31.)

Whatever you do, don't leave this message or anything like it:

You: Oh, hi, Jane, this is Bob from ABC. I just wanted to reach out to you and see if you had any needs in the X, Y, Z area. We provide [yada yada yada]. I certainly would appreciate just a few minutes of your time to talk about your needs. If you get a moment, please return my call. I'm at 555-1212. If you miss me, please let me know a good time to call back. Thanks.

Blah, blah, blah, blah, blah. And then, star, seven, delete. Be honest. You'd delete that too, probably before you got to the end of the message. Almost everyone would. A big part of the reason is the singsongy, fake-sounding tonality people typically use to deliver this kind of message. It's usually like the speaker is made of cotton candy—there's nothing actually there. Another big part of the reason to lean away from a message like that is that it is, in fact, submissive. There is zero authority, zero expertise coming through. Remember what we said about avoiding "Mother may I"? This message doesn't.

Keep it short, sweet, and simple, speak clearly and confidently, and support your message with an email or text message if you can.

- Write out and practice a concise voicemail approach based on the coaching you got in this chapter.

CHAPTER 30

Handling
Inbound Calls

L et's talk a little bit about inbound calls that come to you. These calls can benefit from some of the same structure, and even when they're unexpected, you can still plan for them. Clearly there's an interest, otherwise the person wouldn't be calling. So you don't want to fumble this opportunity.

Here's a sample dialogue that will give you some ideas on how to respond effectively to these calls, identify the pain, and set the next step:

[Ring, ring.]

You: Hi, this is Sarah at Laser Incorporated.

Prospect: Hey, Sarah, this is Crystal over at Glass Works. Hey, I was on your website looking for some laser etching/laser marking equipment. I happened to see the PX9000. Wondering how much that thing is.

You: Sure. Let me see if I can help you, Crystal. Thanks. Let me just bring up a couple of files. Hey, let me make sure I've got your contact information. Crystal, what's your last name?

Prospect: Klear.

You: And your phone number, in case we are disconnected?

This is important, because you want to be able to reach out and reconnect at some point if the prospect does not agree to a next step on this call. Many salespeople do not get this information up front, which usually means there is no way to follow up if the prospect disengages from the call.

Prospect: It's 678-555-1212.

You: 678-555-1212. Sure, Crystal. As I'm bringing this up, do you mind if I ask you a couple of questions to get an understanding of the application, what you'll be using this for? So I can direct you to the right laser and share with you the appropriate information?

Prospect: Yeah, sure. If you can help me there, sure.

And now you're ready to outline some pain indicators and see what the person's response is. From here, this inbound call starts to parallel a call you've placed. You want to understand what motivated this person to make the call and why they are out looking for what you're selling.

Notice what you didn't say. You didn't say, "Oh, the price on that model is $3,000." This may or may not be the right model the person is asking about, and anyway, you don't want to give out pricing information without engaging in some kind of conversation about pain indicators. (You also don't say, "We don't give out that kind of information over the phone," because that's a major turnoff.) The whole idea is to get some contact information, start a discussion between peers, and try to set an appropriate next step—whatever that is in your sales process.

Mark's wife had an experience once in which she called a company looking to buy something, asked the salesperson nine questions in a row, got all the answers she needed, and hung up—all without the salesperson asking for any contact information or making any attempt to set up a next step. She got the information she needed—and then she called the company's biggest competitor. That's not the kind of conversation you want to have on an inbound call.

- Write out and practice an inbound call approach, based on your situation and the coaching you got in this chapter.

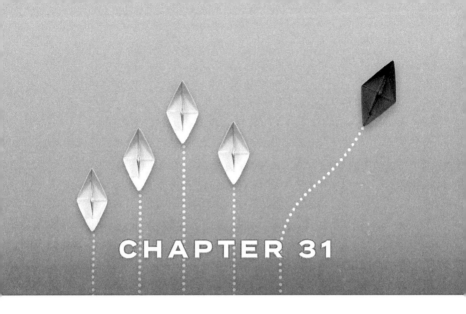

CHAPTER 31

The One-Two Punch and Other Tools to Bridge the Digital Gap

I n this chapter, we return to a point we shared with you in Chapter 1: Salespeople now live in a different world than the one they used to live in.

In this world, buyers are increasingly reliant on digital communication tools that salespeople don't necessarily have access to or even know about. Buyers are increasingly protective of their time and attention. And buyers are increasingly hard to reach voice-to-voice and increasingly wary about talking to salespeople. So here's the question: How can you use your own digital resources to create and hasten the opportunity to engage in a real-time conversation with someone about whether it makes sense for you and them to do business together?

Below are our five favorite answers to this important question. We offer this list with a warning: Things change with extraordinary speed on the digital frontier. There is no way any list of strategies that anyone can offer in this area will stay cutting-edge for long. By definition, we are leaving something important out, something that people just started doing. But what we outline below has worked for us and for our clients up until now.

That said, we are pragmatists. We don't suggest that any one of these ideas is authoritative, guaranteed to work in your market, or likely to match up with your personal style. What we do suggest, though, is that it probably makes sense for you to experiment with all five, to pick two or three that seem likeliest to deliver good results in your market, and then to execute, execute, execute, so you can track what is working and measure how well it is working. When in doubt, do the behaviors—and keep track of the results.

The One-Two Punch

The idea here is that you create two or more touchpoints on a single day, using different platforms, and that you do that once a week. So for instance, if you've got a cell phone number and an email address for Geraldo Garcia of Western Sales, and Geraldo has a LinkedIn profile and a shared connection with your happy client Jennifer Ryan who said you should reach out to Geraldo, your four-week plan for connecting with Geraldo might look like this:

- **Week one:** You call Geraldo and leave a voicemail message briefly referencing your shared contact Jennifer, who thought it might be important that you talk to Geraldo, and you reference the promise you made to her to reach out. Of course, you speak clearly and say your number twice. On the same day, you also send a brief email with the heading "Jennifer Ryan" and you tell Geraldo, in the body of the message, that Jennifer thought it might be important that you speak to him, that you had promised you would reach out, and that is why you are suggesting the two of you talk at such-and-such date and time.
- **Week two.** You leave another voicemail message along the same lines. On the same day, you also send out a LinkedIn request to connect with Geraldo. This request references Jennifer.
- **Week three.** You send Geraldo a brief text message referencing your discussion with Jennifer and suggesting a date and time for a conversation. On the same day, you send a brief email, worded slightly differently from your first email, with the heading "Call on March 15 at 2 P.M.?" (or whatever date and time you are proposing). You do not try to run a guilt trip of any kind on Geraldo for his not having answered your earlier messages. A couple of days after that, you leave a final voicemail message, saying that you are closing the file but you hope you and Geraldo can connect at some point—and, of course, leaving your number twice.

That's nine touches over a 21-day period. We don't recommend that you go beyond that.

This strategy works well for the majority of our clients, and it works well for us, which is why we lead our list with it. The results vary by industry and market, of course, but that's the beauty of what we've just shared with you: You can adapt it easily to any number of situations. We strongly suggest that you give the one-two punch a try because in our experience, it works in virtually any industry; ultimately, of course, you must decide what works in your marketplace and what suits your personal style.

Outsource It

You can outsource the request for an appointment by asking your ally to help you set it up. Here's what that might look like.

Let's assume Jennifer Ryan is one of your first-degree LinkedIn contacts, and you see that she's directly connected to Geraldo Garcia, with whom you want to be connected as well. You send Jennifer an email—not a LinkedIn message, since those are a little more likely to be ignored, but a regular email message—that says something like the following:

> **Email from you:** Hey there, Jennifer, I happened to notice on your LinkedIn profile that you're connected to Geraldo Garcia over at Western Sales. How well do you know him? Would you be willing to introduce me?

Typically, your happy client Jennifer will reply with something like this:

Contact's response: Sure. I know Geraldo very well. He and I went to college together. I'd be happy to introduce you.

Your return email to Jennifer is all-important. That message will say:

Response email from you: Jennifer, I got your message. I really appreciate that. My experience is that an email introduction can work very well for everybody involved. I have attached a template for your review. Please feel free to edit and change it in any way you want.

The template you attach will look like this:

Template from you: Geraldo and [your name], this is Jennifer. I wanted to take the opportunity to introduce the two of you. Geraldo is a good friend of mine, and [your name] is a sales training specialist I have worked with for five years and who does top-notch work. [Your name], I would ask you to reach out to Geraldo and set up a time to speak. If either of you want me to be part of that conversation or have any questions, please reach out. All the best, Jennifer.

Assuming Jennifer approves of your proposed message, or something like it, she will then send the message out to you and to Geraldo. Then you will send an email in response:

Your response to contact and prospect: Hey, Jennifer, thanks so much for the introduction. Geraldo, I'm really looking forward to speaking with you. I'm out of the office on Monday, Tuesday, and Wednesday of this week, but I will be back in on Thursday. I will reach out to you by sending a Zoom invite then. What's a good time to reach you?

You've just set up a Zoom appointment.

Vidyard

Vidyard is another online platform that allows you to spice up your personalized emails to specific individuals by embedding short video messages. It's an incredibly powerful tool you can use not just to leverage personal introductions but also to improve your relationships with existing customers. We highly recommend it. Find out more at vidyard.com.

The Pain-Specific Email

Our colleague Jeremy Thomson, in the UK, has gotten good results for himself and his clients by crafting a highly targeted email that concisely identifies and leverages three very specific pain points that an individual decision maker in a particular, narrowly defined market niche is likely to recognize. He and his clients send variations of that email out to that individual weekly for four weeks, following up via multiple platforms, as outlined in the one-two punch, above.

This is a higher degree of difficulty and complexity, and it takes a fair amount of time to set up, but it may be worth considering if you can manage your time effectively. Just bear in mind that these are highly targeted messages to specific people, not mass email sends. Leave the mass emails to the marketers. They don't work for salespeople.

The LinkedIn Engagement Conversion

This highly effective strategy only works if you make a habit of posting relevant and engaging good content on LinkedIn—and by "good content," we mean content that consistently speaks to one or more of the typical business pains your ideal customer encounters. (That's a habit we would strongly recommend you get into, by the way.) The strategy is breathtakingly simple. Here's how it works.

Someone reads your article or watches your video and engages with it in a positive way.

You then find a way to send that person a very, very brief private message. If you're already connected on LinkedIn or you're using Sales Navigator and the LinkedIn Levers Tool (which we recommend), that's going to be pretty easy to do. Your message should have the heading "Quick question" and read something like this:

> **Your LinkedIn message:** Hey, Geraldo, thanks so much for liking our video. Question: Is Western Sales actively involved in a sales training engagement with our company? [Or any similar question that connects with your industry, such as, "Is Western Sales looking to upgrade or refresh their inventory software this year?"]

People will answer. Try it.

The magic of this technique lies in its brevity. It's almost like you're composing a text message. If you keep it simple and execute this strategy exactly as we have laid it out, you will start a zero-pressure back-and-forth digital dialogue with Geraldo, one that can point you toward a voice-to-voice conversation about whether it makes sense to do business together.

By the way, the same powerful technique can be adapted with ease to the situation where someone visits your website, downloads a white paper, or does something else that fits the profile of your targeted buyer.

This chapter included five powerful options for bridging the digital divide in the 21st century and launching that all-important voice-to-voice discussion. Here's our coaching:

- Leverage all that we have shared with you in the previous chapters.
- Use the tools we have provided for you in the Appendix.
- Then try one or two strategies from the list above that feel best to you and that seem most viable in your market, build them into your cookbook, and start executing.

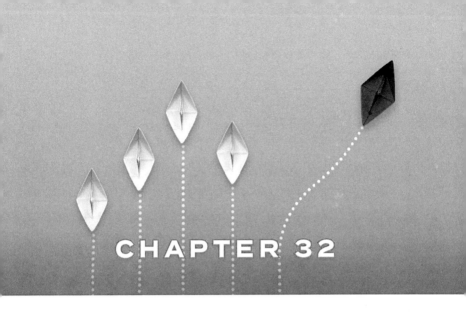

CHAPTER 32

Upgrade Your Belief System

You'll recall the Success Triangle. We've talked in-depth about technique (knowing what to do), and we've talked about behavior (actually doing it). Now, in the final few chapters of this book, it's time to do a deep dive about that third point on the Success Triangle: attitude. This is where the rubber hits the road.

Are You Ready to Upgrade Your Belief System?

Take a close look at this model called the Belief Wheel.

This visual says that beliefs lead to judgments, which in turn lead to actions (or non-actions), which will drive results, which, in turn, will reinforce some of the original beliefs. The bottom line here is that you want to look very closely at what you believe about yourself and others because that is definitely going to have an impact on your prospecting outcomes.

Let's look at a couple of examples of how this might play out, and, just for the sake of clarity, let's take the discussion out of the realm of prospecting for a moment. Let's pretend you're a salesperson who believes the only thing that matters is price. That's all that matters. You're convinced that no one cares about anything else anymore. Just price.

Well, when you're sitting across from a prospect (let's call her Jazmine), what do you believe she thinks? You believe, with zero evidence, that the only thing that matters to Jazmine is price. Why? Because you're not seeing the world the way it is. You're seeing the world the way you are.

> **People don't see the world the way it is.**
> **They see the world the way they are.**

Now if you're a salesperson who believes the only thing that matters is price, and if you're sitting across from Jazmine and you believe she believes the only thing that matters is price, what will you do based on that belief? Just as important, what won't you do, based on that belief?

Here's what you'll do. You'll discount. Without Jazmine even asking you to do so, you'll go in low. You'll negotiate against yourself even before you start talking to her. Why? Because that's your belief system. You believe that "X dollars is where I need to be just to have a shot." That's not what Jazmine told you. That's something you made up on your own.

Now let's look at the second half of that question: What won't you do? Think about that one for a second. It's important.

If you believe that Jazmine is focused only on price, here is a partial list of the things you won't do:

- You won't focus on value. Specifically, you won't focus on the monetary value of the solution that you could deliver to Jazmine.
- You won't focus on the pain that you could remove from Jazmine's world.
- You won't focus on the margin that your organization needs to sustain on every sale in order to operate profitably. That doesn't even exist for you. It's off your radar screen.

You're not focusing on any of those things because to you, they not only don't matter, they don't exist. If they don't exist, why would you focus on them? And since they don't exist, you go in and close a $2,000 sale for $965.

And now what do you say to yourself? To your boss? To your spouse?

Many times, right after salespeople close a sale that's worth a fraction of what it should be, that's when they start telling themselves and other people, "Well, it's not really about price. It's about the relationship. It's about getting in the door. It's about generating good word of mouth, yada yada yada." That's when they try to convince themselves and others that it's not about price.

What the heck were they thinking a half an hour earlier, back when they were talking to the prospect?

This is another example of head trash. Head trash, as we've said, is beliefs that people have that lead to negative outcomes or negative results. There's an old saying that's often attributed to Mark Twain: "It ain't what you don't know that gets you into trouble. It's what you know for sure that just ain't so." That's relevant here. It all starts with your own belief system. It's not what you don't know that hurts you. It's what you know for sure (but that you're wrong about) that really does a number on you.

> Head trash is beliefs that people have that lead
> to negative outcomes or negative results.

Here's another example of the impact of head trash on outcomes. You may or may not know what an invisible fence is: It's a system that sets borders around your yard on where your dog can and can't go, using ultrasound. The system emits a sound that the dog doesn't like, and when the dog hears that sound, it stops in its tracks.

Years ago, coauthor John got a new dog for his family, a beautiful one-year-old golden retriever named Toby. This was back when he had young kids running around the house, so there was a challenge: Every time one of those kids opened up the front door, that dog bolted. John wasted all kinds of time wandering through the neighborhood, looking for that lost dog. It happened multiple times, and frankly, he reached a point where he was sick of it. His loving wife then came to the rescue:

John's wife: Sweetheart, I think we should get a fence. I'm thinking about one of those invisible fences.

John [happy for this great solution]: Sounds great. Let's buy it.

John's wife: What are you doing tonight?

John [suspecting something]: Well, why do you ask, honey?

John's wife: Because I have the invisible fence guy coming over tonight. Can you sit with him?

John: Terrific! What do you think an invisible fence costs?

John's wife: I don't have any idea.

John: If it's less than $3,000, we're buying the fence tonight. Agree?

John's wife: Absolutely. You have no argument here.

Spoiler alert: They're going to find out later that the fence costs $1,000. Now, just to recap, if you're playing along at home: When did John want to buy a fence? That night. How much was he willing to spend? $3,000.

Later that night, the doorbell rings and John and his wife invite the invisible fence salesperson in. He takes a seat in the living room. John takes a seat across from him. John's wife goes into the kitchen. (She likes to leave the heavy lifting for John.)

Right in front of the invisible fence salesperson is a coffee table. The only thing on that coffee table is John's checkbook. It's open. Repeat: The checkbook is open. How much more direct does a buying signal get?

The guy ignores that signal. Instead of asking about the checkbook or anything else of consequence, he delivers this whole carefully choreographed presentation. He tells John all about the features and benefits. The fence has six adjustable RF frequencies. It has this. It has that. John doesn't care. He's waiting for the close, so he can say yes.

In the end, the invisible fence salesperson takes out a piece of paper with names and numbers on it, places it on the coffee table, and says, "Mr. Rosso, here's what I'd like you to do. This sheet has the names, addresses, and phone numbers of people in your neighborhood who have purchased the fence and are satisfied. What I'd like you to do is call them and if you're still interested, call me."

And with that, he gathers up his stuff, stands up, and leaves. Quickly.

John is stunned. The salesperson is out the door before John has the chance to say anything to stop him. It's like he's running for his life. John's wife comes in from the kitchen, sees that the guy has left, and says, "What did you do? Did you buy the fence?"

"No, he wouldn't let me!" John is left with the puzzling question, *Why didn't I buy a fence just now?*

What do you think that salesperson's belief was about selling a $1,000 fence to a couple on the first night he meets them? *Never going to happen.*

That was head trash. Do you see it?

Based on that head trash, what was his judgment about John? *This guy's never going to buy.*

John literally had a checkbook on the table throughout this entire discussion. What actions (or, more accurately, non-actions) did this salesperson take in response to that? He didn't even ask about it!

And what were the results? That gentleman walked out on the easiest sale of his life.

Not only that, he created a self-fulfilling prophecy. He strengthened his own (off-kilter) belief system. Because of that belief system, John and his wife did not buy a fence that night—and they were as ready to buy as human beings can get.

Now, put yourself in that salesperson's seat. This isn't really about him. It's about all salespeople. If you really want to make a change, if you really want to get rid of the head trash, what has to change first? Your beliefs or your actions?

Most people say beliefs. But here's the right answer: your actions. You need to devise a different behavior, a different action.

Follow this through: What could he have done differently

to get John to buy the fence for $3,000? (By the way, If you're thinking he should have asked, "What's your budget?" give yourself a demerit. That's not the question he wanted to ask, because surprise, surprise, John would've lied. John didn't want to spend a lot of money if he didn't have to.)

To close that sale on the spot for maybe three times the list price, that invisible fence salesperson could have simply said, just as soon as he sat down, "I'm trying to understand, why are you folks looking for a fence?"

If he'd asked that question, some fascinating things would have happened. John would have probably broken down and cried in gratitude. John would definitely have said that he wanted to wrap this up as quickly as possible. He would also have said that his wife had heard great things about this fence from one of the neighbors and that they both wanted it installed tomorrow morning if possible. John would have told the invisible fence salesperson that he didn't ever want to have to go searching through the neighborhood for a lost dog again. It would have (or it should have) become clear to the salesperson, as the conversation continued, that John was willing to pay a premium price for an expedited fence that really did make wandering around the neighborhood in search of a golden retriever a thing of the past.

None of that happened. Why? Because this salesperson had head trash. He had bought into a set of beliefs that did not support anyone.

Again, what changes first: your beliefs or your actions? Invariably, we find that most people we talk to about this think it's beliefs. Actually, it's the choice to take an action that moves you out of your comfort zone that winds up changing your belief system. If you just sit in the basement and say to yourself for hours on end, "I hate reaching out to strangers, I hate reaching out to strangers, I hate reaching out to strangers," and you wait for that belief about strangers to change, when will you make your first call? Never!

The Big Takeaway

Here's the big takeaway. The rule we want you to follow about beliefs is a simple one: You cannot let the way you feel control the way you act. Instead, you've got to let the way you act control the way you feel.

By definition, when you're acting outside of your comfort zone, you're acting in the opposite direction of your head-trash belief. That's a good thing. As the saying goes, you've got to feel the fear and do it anyway. You've got to make the commitment to do what you said you would do, regardless of how you feel at the moment. You've got to keep an eagle-eye out for head trash so you can identify it for what it is and take the opposite action whenever you come across it.

> You cannot let the way you feel control the way you act. Instead, you've got to let the way you act control the way you feel.

Many people grew up with loving parents who told them never to talk to strangers. Maybe you're one of those people. Do you now hold, at some level or other, the belief that talking to strangers is dangerous? This is head trash.

Stop and think for a moment: How would a belief like this hold you back as a sales professional, if you did have it? What kinds of actions would you take if you held a different belief, the belief that there is opportunity in every new conversation with every new person you meet? How could you change your actions to change the beliefs you held, the judgments you made, and the results you produced around the issue of talking to strangers?

- Take an inventory of your belief system. Identify specific beliefs that may be keeping you from executing your prospecting plan. Write down the top two or three pieces of head trash (like, "talking to strangers is dangerous") that may be holding you back right now.
- Ask yourself: "Who is someone who believes differently from me about this issue, who gets different or better results? What do they do differently? What could I be doing that they do?"
- Then, focus on the things you can control—and take action. Let the way you act begin to control the way you feel.

Nothing Personal

A while back, Mark was watching television, flipping through channels, when he came across an interview with the actor George Clooney. Mark put down the remote when he heard the interviewer ask Clooney about his early days, the days when he was not yet George Clooney, movie star, but a struggling actor waiting tables, trying to get a gig. Something told Mark that what he was about to hear connected with the discipline of prospecting. He was right.

Clooney told the interviewer about one time in particular when he was going into an audition for a big role. On this particular occasion, he was really nervous. He had, for months, been having a hard time landing jobs, and there had been a very long stretch where he was not bringing in the income he wanted from his acting. He was feeling down about all of that. And then, on his way into this one audition, something changed.

Clooney said that a switch flipped in his head as he got ready to audition for this role. Clooney said, "You know, if you think about it, every time you go on an audition, you're playing with house money. From the minute you walk in, you don't have the job, to the minute you walk out, you don't have the job. Nothing is different. The only thing that can be different is you get the job. If you think of it that way, you take off all the pressure. The worst thing that can happen is I don't get a job I already don't have."

He went on to explain that once he looked at the audition that way, he suddenly felt as though he was playing in Vegas with house money. After all, the worst thing that could possibly happen was that he would walk out without a job that he already didn't have. And the upside was spectacular.

This was the point at which his career turned around. This was the point at which he started getting roles. He stopped taking rejection personally and began to see what he was doing as all upside.

The Clooney Principle

Why do we tell you a story about an actor? Because if you can take that same mindset and apply it to prospecting, you can make the same kind of breakthrough.

What's the worst thing that can possibly happen when you do one of your prospecting behaviors? Nothing. Stop and think about that. That's not so bad. The worst thing that happens when you prospect is you don't get something you already don't have. What's the best thing that can happen? You get an appointment, you get a meeting, you get an introduction. So many good things can happen. The fact is, when you start to think like that, you're playing with house money. Call it the Clooney Principle.

That's the mindset you need to have: The worst thing that can happen is you don't get something you already didn't have. House money!

So for those times you might take things personally and feel rejected when prospecting, think about this: Have you ever seen a boxing match or a mixed martial arts fight? Two people in the ring are beating each other down, hammering each other left and right and center. At the end of every fight, what do they do? Right after the last bell rings, something extraordinary takes place. The two fighters who have been beating the daylights out of each other go to the middle of the ring—and they hug each other.

They understand something important, something that is good to learn in sales and particularly in prospecting. Those boxers understand that what they've been doing in the ring is just part of the job.

It's a role that they're playing. When one fighter hits the other in the face, you'd think the second guy would take that personally, but most of the time, they don't. They don't because they know that the behavior is expected. It's part of the role.

Now, let's apply that attitude to sales and to prospecting. There are going to be times when you're going to get thrown a punch (figuratively, we hope). You're going to take it on the chin. What you need to understand is that it's not an assault on you personally. It's only an attack on the role you happen to be playing on that particular day.

If you allow those things to start to affect you, if you allow yourself to take it personally, that's going to really hurt your self-esteem. It's going to hurt how you feel about yourself. As a result of that damage, your performance is going to suffer. You're not going to prospect again or prospect as much. You're also not going to have the posture and presence and confidence you need in order to succeed.

You want to be like the boxers in that ring. You want to get good at reminding yourself, "Hey, it's just a job. It's just part of the role."

This brings us to an important topic, the topic of identity and role separation. That's what we'll be looking at in the next chapter. For now, though, be sure to do the assignment you see below.

- Think of a time when something challenging happened to you as a result of you performing your role as a professional salesperson—a time when you took a punch, as it were. It could be someone speaking to you rudely or swearing at you. It could be someone hanging up on you. It could be someone saying no after you'd put a lot of work into a relationship. The only criteria here are:

- It happened when you were doing your job;
- It involved an interaction with another person; and
- You didn't enjoy it.

- Have you got an incident in mind? Good.
- Now ask yourself: Did you take that event personally, even a little?
- If so, why? Was that event really about you? Or was it about the role you were playing at that moment?

CHAPTER 34

Identity and Role Separation

There's an old-time story from the 1950s about a boy named Barney who goes to the big high school dance. Barney wants to dance with his crush, Katie, but he's too afraid to ask her. (Many people, then and now, have been in that position.)

Hours go by, and Barney can't manage to work up his nerve. Finally, after much goading from his buddies, he is encouraged to walk that 50 feet across the gymnasium floor to ask Katie to dance.

He makes it to the other side of the gym, and he says, "Katie, would you like to dance?"

Katie takes one look at Barney and says, "No, thanks."

Now think about how long that walk back took. It felt like forever! Barney makes a vow, "I will never do that again."

Why? Because he took it on the identity side. Barney felt like he didn't just fail in his role as a dance-getter. He felt like he failed as a person, and he wanted to avoid the pain of that kind of failure ever coming back for a return engagement. In fact, he felt like he'd do just about anything to avoid that pain.

Fast-forward three months. Next big school dance. Barney is there and his buddy Fred is there. Katie is there, too, in the same spot, all the way on the other side of the gym. Fred leans in and says to Barney, "Hey, do you still have a crush on Katie?"

Barney says, "You bet."

Fred has an idea. He says, "Why don't I go ask her to dance for you?" Barney agrees to this. So now Fred walks that same 50 feet across the dance floor. How long does that 50 feet feel to him? It feels like 50 feet.

Fred says, "Hey, Katie, do you want to dance with my buddy Barney?"

"No, thanks." Nothing's changed.

Fred is a good friend. He works his way right down the line.

"Hey Becky, would you want to dance with my buddy Barney?"

"No."

"Aw, c'mon. Take a look at him."

"I did. Cannot happen."

"Hey, Stephanie, how about you?"

"You've got to be kidding."

Fred keeps getting rejected. He can't manage to get a dance

for Barney. Now, here's a question for you: When Fred walks the same 50 feet across the gym floor to get back to his buddy Barney, what is he saying to himself? Is he saying, "I'm a failure"? No! He's saying, "It ain't me—the problem is that I've got a bad product to sell!"

Fred comes out best in this story because he's managed to separate the identity from the role. And they just have to wait until Barney finds Betty.

Here's the moral: If you take failure personally, that's a problem because it stops you from taking risks. The bigger the risk you take, the more likely you are to feel that, if something goes wrong, it won't be the role that's failing. It will be you as an individual. And nobody wants that feeling.

The Desert Island

Here's another thought exercise. Let's pretend you're on a desert island. (You're only going to be there for a few minutes.) Assume that you leave all of your roles behind and you're sitting there by yourself. You're not a parent, you're not someone's child, you're not a salesperson or a Scout club leader. You're just you. Got it?

Great. Now rate your identity on a scale of 1 to 10. One is low, 10 high. Take a moment. Do it now. Rate the *you* who is left without any role to play.

John knows what he wrote down years ago. He wrote down a seven. When people asked him why, he said, "Well, I'm not perfect. I'm not the greatest expert at anything. I guess I have a lot of room to grow." Now, though, he knows: None of that matters.

Here's the truth. Your identity is who you are. And who you are is perfect, right now. That's true for everyone. Your "R," your role, may go up and down. But your "I" is always a 10 out of 10.

Once you come to understand that, you become bullet-proof. You can be vulnerable on the outside and strong on the inside. You can bounce back easily from anything a prospect or a buyer throws at you. Perhaps you are thinking right now that this sounds very nice in theory, but it sounds impossible for you to put into practice. Perhaps you are wondering how you could possibly hold that kind of understanding of yourself, the understanding of yourself as a 10 out of 10. It may happen through small steps at first. Start by accepting that when you experience rejection or failure or any kind of negative outcome, that failure isn't you.

You may have failed in your role, but *you* aren't a failure. You always have the ability to step back, take a deep breath, and understand, at the core of your being, that you are a 10. We've got a saying at our company: "They can take a piece of your armor, but they can't take a piece of you."

Looking for a way to improve your performance in any (and we do mean any) role? Get back on the horse and remind your-self that you are an "I"-10. People perform consistently with how they see themselves conceptually. So, change how you see yourself. Take action. Work on your "I" (your identity), and your "R" (your roles) will take off.

> People perform consistently with how they see themselves conceptually.

- Write down a positive thought or affirmation that you can use to strengthen yourself any time you think you feel your "I" slipping. For instance: "I take action in the face of fear."
- Post this where you will see it regularly. Then, take action!
- You cannot go wrong if you follow the advice David Sandler shared with John years ago and, by extension, through resources like this book, is still sharing with sales professionals today:

"Do the behaviors! Do the behaviors! Do the behaviors!"

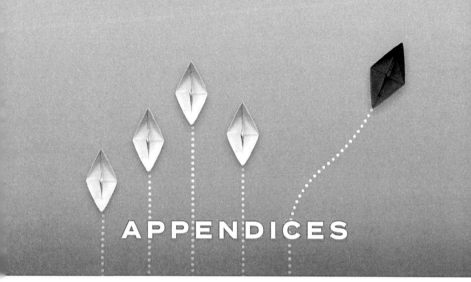

APPENDICES

Download editable versions of the Tools
featured on the following pages for free at
Sandler.com/21stCenturyProspecting

── BUSINESS DEVELOPMENT TOOLS ✖ ──

LinkedIn® Levers Tool

Researching the client: _____

Do you have any mutual connections with the client?

How many connections does the client have?

Which college attended and degree attained?

What is the client's hometown and current city?

Where did the client work previously?

How much time did the client spend at previous jobs?

Which companies and groups does the client follow

What type of info does the client post/share? Which influencers does he follow?

What activities and interests does the client list?

To which industry groups does the client belong?

Does the client endorse others? Is he endorsed often and for what?

Has the client been recommended by anyone? If so, by whom?

Does the client support any charities or initiatives?

Researching the company: _____

How does the company present itself in its profile? Are there any key themes?

What competitors are identified in the company's "also viewed" section?

Do you have any connections with former employees?

Is the company currently hiring full-time employees? In what areas?

What key products/services does the company highlight in its profile?

Can you identify any connections after scrolling through the company's employee list?

BUSINESS DEVELOPMENT TOOLS ✖

QVR Tool

1. Attendees

Client Firm: **Our Firm:**

2. Client-Centric Satisfaction

Satisfaction Factor	Rating	Comment	Reset Factor

Rating Scale: 1. Corrective Action Needed   2. Improvement Needed   3. Acceptable   4. Good   5. Excellent

3. Service Scoreboard

KPI	Performance	Reset Factor

—— BUSINESS DEVELOPMENT TOOLS ✗ ——

QVR Tool

4. Service Improvement

Previous Improvement Action	Result	New Improvement Action

5. Impacts

Client/Industry/Market Impact	Action Plan

6. Strategic Innovation

Idea	Action Plan

BUSINESS DEVELOPMENT TOOLS ✗

The 30-Second Commercial Creator

HEADLINE & STORY

With whom do you work? (Roles or Companies)

-
-
-
-
-

Top 4 issues (pains) prospects have (or complain about) that you can solve:

Headlines

1.

2.

3.

4.

Trigger Phrases:

-
-
-
-

- Stay behind the pendulum.
- Focus on the prospect, not the seller.
- Keep it brief.

1. _____ which means
   -
   -
   -

2. _____ which means
   -
   -
   -

3. _____ which means
   -
   -
   -

4. _____ which means
   -
   -
   -

Negative Reverse:

1.

2.

3.

4.

BUSINESS DEVELOPMENT TOOLS ✗

The 30-Second Commercial Creator

CREATE YOUR BASIC 30-SECOND COMMERCIAL

Use words and phrases that YOU would actually say!

Introduction

Who you are, the name of your company and briefly what your company does

Pain Statement

Positive emotional word with an opportunity or a negative emotional word with a problem/challenge (Headlines)

Benefit Statement

A simple acknowledgement of helping others with these issues

Hook/Pendulum Statement or Question

Remember to stay behind the pendulum and assume prospects **don't** have these issues

The 30-Second Commercial Creator

CREATE YOUR BASIC 30-SECOND COMMERCIAL

Use words and phrases that YOU would actually say!

Based on Behavioral Style	Dominant	Influencer	Steady Relator	Compliant
Introduction Who you are, the name of your company and briefly what your company does				
Pain Statement Positive emotional word with an opportunity or a negative emotional word with a problem/challenge (Headlines)				
Benefit Statement A simple acknowledgement of helping others with these issues				
Hook/Pendulum Statement or Question Remember to stay behind the pendulum and assume prospects **don't** have these issues				

— BUSINESS DEVELOPMENT TOOLS ✖ —

The Cookbook Creator

You can't build a prospecting plan without first determining what you want to accomplish.

My Monthly Financial Goal   _____

My Average Monthly Salary   _____   **Divide Your Monthly Financial Goal by Your Average Commission to arrive at the number of Sales Needed Each Month!**

Amount of Commission Needed Each Month   _____

Commission Earned on an Average Deal   _____

Number of **Deals** Needed Each Month   _____

Number of **Presentations** Needed to Close One Sale?   _____

Number of **Initial Meetings** Needed to get 1 Presentation Opportunity?   _____

Number of **Contacts** Needed to get One Initial Meeting?   _____

Number of **Attempts** to get One Contact?   _____

The ONLY Thing You Can CONTROL!

Attempts ÷
of Working Days
= MDB

Number of Working Days This Month   _____

MINIMUM DAILY BEHAVIOR   _____

Look for these other books on shop.sandler.com:

SALES SERIES

The Art and Skill of Sales Psychology

Asking Questions the Sandler Way

Bootstrap Selling the Sandler Way

Call Center Success the Sandler Way

The Contrarian Salesperson

Digital Prospecting

Gold Medal Selling

LinkedIn the Sandler Way

Prospect the Sandler Way

Retail Success in an Online World

Sandler Enterprise Selling

The Sandler Rules

The Unapologetic Saleswoman

Why People Buy

You Can't Teach a Kid to
Ride a Bike at a Seminar

MANAGEMENT & LEADERSHIP SERIES

Change the Sandler Way

Customer Service the Sandler Way

The Intentional Sales Manager

Lead When You Dance

Motivational Management
the Sandler Way

Making the Climb

Misery to Mastery

The Right Hire

The Road to Excellence

The Sales Coach's Playbook

The Sandler Rules for Sales Leaders

The Success Cadence

Transforming Leaders
the Sandler Way

Winning from Failing

21st Century Ride Along

Scaling Sales Success

PROFESSIONAL DEVELOPMENT SERIES

Accountability the Sandler Way

From the Board Room to
the Living Room

Goal-Setting Boot Camp

Negotiating From the Inside Out

Sandler Success Principles

Succeed the Sandler Way

INDUSTRY SERIES

Making Channel Sales Work

Patient Care the Sandler Way

Selling in Manufacturing
and Logistics

Selling Professional Services
the Sandler Way

Selling to Homeowners
the Sandler Way

Selling Technology the Sandler Way

FREE VIDEO LESSON:

SELLING IN A
HYBRID WORLD

To access a complimentary video lesson from HubSpot and Sandler, SELLING IN A HYBRID WORLD, and learn what it takes to move your current sales process into a hybrid model, visit:

sandler.com/hybridselling